THE MOVING PICTURE GIRLS

OR

First Appearances in Photo Dramas

LAURA LEE HOPE

The Moving Picture Girls

Laura Lee Hope

PO Box 2211
Fairfield, IA 52556
www.1stworldlibrary.com
First Edition

LCCN: 2006935243

Softcover ISBN: 1-4218-2496-5
Hardcover ISBN: 1-4218-2396-9
eBook ISBN: 1-4218-2596-1

1st World Library Literary Society

Giving Back to the World

"If you want to work on the core problem, it's early school literacy."

- James Barksdale, former CEO of Netscape

"No skill is more crucial to the future of a child, or to a democratic and prosperous society, than literacy."

- Los Angeles Times

Literacy... means far more than learning how to read and write... The aim is to transmit... knowledge and promote social participation."

- UNESCO

"Literacy is not a luxury, it is a right and a responsibility. If our world is to meet the challenges of the twenty-first century we must harness the energy and creativity of all our citizens."

- President Bill Clinton

"Parents should be encouraged to read to their children, and teachers should be equipped with all available techniques for teaching literacy, so the varying needs and capacities of individual kids can be taken into account."

- Hugh Mackay

CONTENTS

CHAPTER I

AN UNCEREMONIOUS DEPARTURE

"Oh, isn't it just splendid, Ruth? Don't you feel like singing and dancing? Come on, let's have a two-step! I'll whistle!"

"Alice! How can you be so - so boisterous?" expostulated the taller of two girls, who stood in the middle of their small and rather shabby parlor.

"Boisterous! Weren't you going to say - rude?" laughingly asked the one who had first spoken. "Come, now, 'fess up! Weren't you?" and the shorter of the twain, a girl rather plump and pretty, with merry brown eyes, put her arm about the waist of her sister and endeavored to lead her through the maze of chairs in the whirl of a dance, whistling, meanwhile, a joyous strain from one of the latest Broadway successes.

"Oh, Alice!" came in rather fretful tones. "I don't -"

"You don't know what to make of me? That's it; isn't it, sister mine? Oh, I can read you like a book. But, Ruth, why aren't you jolly once in a while? Why always that 'maiden all forlorn' look on your face? Why that far-away, distant look in your eyes - 'Anne, Sister Anne, dost see anyone approaching?' Talk about Bluebeard! Come on, do one turn with me. I'm learning the one-step, you know, and it's lovely!

"Come on, laugh and sing! Really, aren't you glad that dad has an engagement at last? A real engagement that will bring in some real money! Aren't you glad? It will mean so much to us! Money! Why, I haven't seen enough real money of late to have a speaking acquaintance with it. We've been trusted for everything, except carfare, and it would have come to that pretty soon. Say you're glad, Ruth!"

The younger girl gave up the attempt to entice her sister into a dance, and stood facing her, arm still about her waist, the laughing brown eyes gazing mischievously up into the rather sad blue ones of the taller girl.

"Glad? Of course I'm glad, Alice DeVere, and you know it. I'm just as glad as you are that daddy has an engagement. He's waited long enough for one, goodness knows!"

"You have a queer way of showing your gladness," commented the other drily, shrugging her shapely shoulders. "Why, I can hardly keep still. La-la-la-la! La-la-la-la! La-la-la!" She hummed the air of a Viennese waltz song, meanwhile whirling gracefully about with extended arms, her dress floating about her balloonwise.

"Oh, Alice! Don't!" objected her sister.

"Can't help it, Ruth. I've just got to dance. La-la!"

She stopped suddenly as a vase crashed to the floor from a table, shattering into many pieces.

"Oh!" cried Alice, aghast, as she stood looking at the ruin she had unwittingly wrought. "Oh, dear, and daddy was so fond of that vase!"

"There, you see what you've done!" exclaimed Ruth, who, though only seventeen, and but two years older than her sister, was of a much more sedate disposition. "I told you not to dance!"

"You did nothing of the sort, Ruth DeVere. You just stood and looked at me, and you wouldn't join in, and maybe if you had this wouldn't have happened - and - and -"

She did not finish, her voice trailing off rather dismally as she stooped to pick up the pieces of the vase.

"It can't be mended, either," she went on, and when she looked up the merry brown eyes were veiled in a mist of tears. Ruth's heart softened at once.

"There, dear!" she said in consoling tones. "Of course you couldn't help it. Don't worry. Daddy won't mind when you tell him you were just doing a little waltz of happiness because he has an engagement at last."

She, too, stooped and her light hair mingled with the dark brown tresses of her sister as they gathered up the fragments.

"I don't care!" announced Alice, finally, as she sank into a chair. "I'll tell dad myself. I'm glad, anyhow, even if the vase is broken. I never liked it. I don't see why dad set such store by the old thing."

"You forget, Alice, that it was one of -"

"Mother's - yes, I know," and she sighed. "Father gave it to her when they were married, but really, mother was like me - she never cared for it."

"Yes, Alice, you are much as mother was," returned Ruth, with gentle dignity. "You are growing more like her every day."

"Am I, really?" and in delight the younger girl sprang up, her grief over the vase for the moment forgotten. "Am I really like her, Ruth? I'm so glad! Tell me more of her. I scarcely remember her. I was only seven when she died, Ruth."

"Eight, my dear. You were eight years old, but such a tiny little thing! I could hold you in my arms."

"You couldn't do it now!" laughed Alice, with a downward glance at her plump figure. Yet she was not over-plump, but with the rounding curves and graces of coming womanhood.

"Well, I couldn't hold you long," laughed Ruth. "But I wonder what is keeping daddy? He telephoned that he would come right home. I'm so anxious to have him tell us all about it!"

"So am I. Probably he had to stay to arrange about rehearsals," replied Alice. "What theater did he say he was going to open at?"

"The New Columbia. It's one of the nicest in New York, too."

"Oh, I'm so glad. Now we can go to a play once in a while - I'm almost starved for the sight of the footlights, and to hear the orchestra tuning up. And you know, while he had no engagement dad wouldn't let us take advantage of his professional privilege, and present his card at the box office."

"Yes, I know he is peculiar that way. But I shall be glad, too, to attend a play now and again. I'm getting quite rusty. I did so want to see Maude Adams when she was here. But -"

"I'd never have gone in the dress I had!" broke in Alice. "I want something pretty to wear; don't you?"

"Of course I do, dear. But with things the way they were -"

"We had to eat our prospective dresses," laughed Alice. "It was like being shipwrecked, when the sailors have to cut their boots into lengths and make a stew of them."

"Alice!" cried Ruth, rather shocked.

"It was so!" affirmed the other. "Why, you must have read of it dozens of times in those novels you're always poring over. The hero and heroine on a raft - she looks up into his eyes and sighs. 'Have another morsel of boot soup, darling!' Why, the time dad had to use the money he had half promised me for that charmeuse, and we bought the supper at the delicatessen - you know, when Mr. Blake stopped and you asked him to stay to tea, when there wasn't a thing in the house to eat - do you remember that?"

"Yes, but I don't see what it has to do with shipwrecked sailors eating their boots. Really, Alice -"

"Of course it was just the same," explained the younger girl, merrily. "There was nothing fit to give Mr. Blake, and I took the money that was to have been paid for my charmeuse, and slipped out to Mr. Dinkelspatcher's - or whatever his name is - and bought a meal. Well, we ate my dress, that's all, Ruth."

"Why, Alice!"

"And I wish we had it to eat over again," went on the other, with a half sigh. "I don't know what we are going to do for supper. How much have we in the purse?"

"Only a few dollars."

"And we must save that, I suppose, until dad gets some salary, which won't be for a time yet. And we really ought to celebrate in some way, now that he's had this bit of good luck! Oh, isn't it just awful to be poor!"

"Hush, Alice! The neighbors will hear you. The walls of this apartment house are so terribly thin!"

"I don't care if they do hear. They all know dad hasn't had a theatrical engagement for ever so long. And they know we haven't any what you might call - resources - or we wouldn't live here. Of course they know we're poor - that's no news!"

"I know, my dear. But you are so - so out-spoken."

"I'm glad of it. Oh, Ruth, when will you ever give up trying to pretend we are what we are not? You're a dear, nice, sweet, romantic sister, and some day I hope the Fairy Prince will come riding past on his milk-white steed - and, say, Ruth, why should a prince always ride a milk-white steed? There's something that's never been explained.

"All the novels and fairy stories have milk-white steeds for the hero to prance up on when he rescues the doleful maiden. And if there's any color that gets dirtier sooner, and makes a horse look most like a lost hope, it's white. Of course I know they can keep a circus horse milk-white, but it isn't practical for princes or heroes. The first mud puddle he splashed through - And, oh, say! If the prince should fail in his fortunes later, and have to hire out to drive a coal wagon! Wouldn't his milk-white steed look sweet then? There goes one now," and she pointed out of the window to the street below.

"Do, Ruth, if your prince comes, insist on his changing his steed for one of sober brown. It will wear better."

"Don't be silly, Alice!"

"Oh, I can't help it. Hark, is that dad's step?"

The two girls listened, turning their heads toward the hall entrance door.

"No, it's someone over at the Dalwoods' - across the corridor."

The noise in the hallway increased. There were hasty footsteps, and then rather loud voices.

"I tell you I won't have anything to do with you, and you needn't come sneaking around here any more. I'm done with you!"

"That's Russ," whispered Alice.

"Yes," agreed Ruth, and her sister noted a slight flush on her fair cheeks.

Then came a voice in expostulation:

"But I tell you I can market it for you, and get you something for it. If you try to go it alone -"

"Well, that's just what I'm going to do - go it alone, and I don't want to hear any more from you. Now you get out!"

"But look here -"

There was a sound of a scuffle, and a body crashed up against the door of the DeVere apartment.

"Oh!" cried Ruth and Alice together.

Their door swung open, for someone had seemingly caught at the knob to save himself from falling. The girls had a glimpse of their neighbor across the hall, Russ Dalwood by name, pushing a strange man toward the head of the stairs.

"Now you get out!" cried Russ, and the man left rather unceremoniously, slipping down two or three steps before he could recover his balance and grasp the railing.

"Oh, shut the door, quickly, Alice!" gasped Ruth.

CHAPTER II

RUSS DALWOOD APOLOGIZES

The portal was closed with a bang - so closed because Alice in a mad rush threw herself against it and turned the key in the lock. Then she gained a place by her sister's side, and slipped an arm about her waist.

"He - he won't come in," Alice whispered. "I saw him going down the stairs."

"Who - who was it?" faltered Ruth. She was very pale.

"I don't know," Alice made answer. "I don't believe he meant to come in here. It was - was just an accident. But the door is locked now. Maybe it was some collector - like those horrid men who have been to see us lately. The Dalwoods may be short of money, too."

"I don't think so, Alice. Russ makes good wages at the moving picture place. Oh, are you sure the door is locked?"

"Positive. Don't worry."

"Let's slip down the back stairs to Mrs. Reilley's flat. She has a telephone, and we can call the police," suggested the taller girl, in a hoarse whisper, her eyes never leaving the hall door that had been so unceremoniously thrust open.

"Silly!" returned Alice. "There's no danger now. That man has gone. I tell you I saw him hurrying down the stairs. Russ sent him about his business, all right - whatever his business was."

"Oh, it's terrible to live this way!" wailed Ruth. "With - with common fighting going on in the halls! If poor mother were alive now -"

"She wouldn't be a bit afraid, if what you tell me of her is true!" insisted Alice, stoutly. "And I'm not a bit afraid, either. Why, Russ is just across the hall, and it was only the other day you were saying how strong and manly he was. Have you forgotten?"

"No," answered Ruth, in a low voice, and again the blush suffused her cheeks.

"Then don't be a silly. I'm not going down and ask Mrs. Reilley to 'phone for the police. That would cause excitement indeed. I don't believe anyone else heard the commotion, and that was only because our door flew open by accident."

"Oh, well, maybe it will be all right," assented the taller girl who, in this emergency, seemed to lean on her younger sister. Perhaps it was because Alice was so merry-hearted - even unthinking at times; despising danger because she did not know exactly what it was - or what it meant. Yet even now Ruth felt that she must play the part of mother to her younger sister.

"Are you sure that door is locked?" she asked again.

"Positive! See, I'll slip on the chain, and then it would tax even a policeman to get in. But, really, Ruth, I wouldn't go to Mrs. Reilley's if I were you. She'll tell everyone, and there doesn't seem to be any need. It's all over, and those below, or above us, seem to have heard nothing of it."

"Oh, I wish daddy would come home!"

"So do I, for that matter. That's sensible. What did he say," asked Alice, "when you went down to Mrs. Reilley's telephone to talk to him?" For that neighbor had summoned one of the girls when she learned, over the wire, that Mr. DeVere wished to speak with his daughters about his good fortune.

"He didn't have time to say much," replied Ruth. "He just stole a minute or two away from the conference to say that he had an engagement that was very promising."

"And didn't he say when he'd be home?"

"No, only that it would be as soon as possible."

"Well, I suppose he'll come as quickly as he can. Let's see what we can get up in the way of a lunch. We may have to resort to the delicatessen again. I do want father to have something nice when he comes home with his good news."

"So do I," agreed Ruth. "I'm afraid our ice box doesn't contain much in the way of refreshments for an impromptu banquet, though, and I positively won't go out after - after what happened. At least not right away!"

"Pooh, I'm not afraid!" laughed Alice, having recovered her spirits. "On the ice box - charge!" she cried gaily, waltzing about.

The girls found little enough to reward them, and it came, finally, to the necessity of making a raid on the nearest delicatessen shop if they were to "banquet" their father.

In fact since the DeVere family had come to make their home in the Fenmore Apartment House, on one of the West Sixtieth streets of New York City, there had been very little in the way of food luxuries, and not a great deal of the necessities.

Their life had held a little more of ease and comfort when they lived in a more fashionable quarter, but with the loss of their father's theatrical engagement, and the long period of waiting for another, their savings had been exhausted and they had had recourse to the pawn shop, in addition to letting as many bills as possible go unpaid until fortune smiled again.

Hosmer DeVere, who was a middle-aged, rather corpulent and exceedingly kind and cultured gentleman, was the father of the two girls. Their mother had been dead about seven years, a cold caught in playing on a draughty stage developing into pneumonia, from which she never rallied.

Ruth and Alice came of a theatrical family - at least, on their father's side - for his father and grandfather before him had enviable histrionic reputations. Mrs. DeVere had been a vivacious country maid - or, rather, a maid in a small town that was classed as being on the "country" circuit by the company playing it. Mr. DeVere, then blossoming into a leading man, was in the troupe, and became acquainted with his future wife through the medium of the theater. She had sought an interview with the manager, seeking a chance to "get on the boards," and Mr. DeVere admired her greatly.

Their married life was much happier than the usual theatrical union, and under the guidance and instruction of her husband Mrs. DeVere had become one of the leading juvenile players. Both her husband and herself were fond of home life, and they had looked forward to the day when they could retire and shut themselves away from the public with their two little daughters.

But fortunes are seldom made on the stage - not half as often as is imagined - and the time seemed farther and farther off. Then came Mrs. DeVere's illness and death, and for a time a broken-hearted man withdrew himself from the world to devote his life to his daughters.

But the call of the stage was imperative, not so much from choice as necessity, for Mr. DeVere could do little to advantage save act, and in this alone could he make a living. So he had returned to the "boards," filling various engagements with satisfaction, and taking his daughters about with him.

Rather strange to say, up to the present, though literally saturated with the romance and hard work of the footlights, neither Ruth nor Alice had shown any desire to go on the stage. Or, if they had it, they had not spoken of it. And their father was glad.

Mr. DeVere was a clever character actor, and had created a number of parts that had won favor. He inclined to whimsical comedy roles, rather than to romantic drama, and several of his old men studies are remembered on Broadway to this day. He had acted in Shakespeare, but he had none of that burning desire, with which many actors are credited, to play Hamlet. Mr. DeVere was satisfied to play the legitimate in his best manner, to look after his daughters, and to trust that in time he might lay by enough for himself, and see them happily married.

But the laying-aside process had been seriously interrupted several times by lack of engagements, so that the little stock of savings dwindled away.

Then came a panicky year. Many theaters were closed, and more actors "walked the Rialto" looking for engagements than ever before. Mr. DeVere was among them, and he even accepted a part in a vaudeville sketch to eke out a scanty livelihood.

Good times came again, but did not last, and finally it looked to the actor as though he were doomed to become a "hack," or to linger along in some stock company. He was willing to do this, though, for the sake of the girls.

A rather longer period of inactivity than usual made a decided change in the DeVere fortunes, if one can call a struggle against poverty "fortunes." They had to leave their pleasant apartment and take one more humble. Some of their choice possessions, too, went to the sign of the three golden balls; but, with all this, it was hard work to set even their scanty table. And the bills!

Ruth wept in secret over them, being the house-keeper. And, of late, some of the tradesmen were not as patient and kind as they had been at first. Some even sent professional collectors, who used all their various wiles to humiliate their debtors.

But now a ray of light seemed to shine through the gloom, and a tentative promise from one theatrical manager had become a reality. Mr. DeVere had telephoned that the contract was signed, and that he would have a leading part at last, after many weeks of idleness.

"What is the play?" asked Alice of her sister, when they had decided on what they might safely get from the delicatessen store. "Did dad say?"

"Yes. It's 'A Matter of Friendship.' One of those new society dramas."

"Oh, I do hope he gets us tickets!"

"We will need some dresses before we can use tickets," sighed Ruth. "Positively I wouldn't go anywhere but in the gallery now."

"No, we wouldn't exactly shine in a box," agreed Alice.

"Hark!" cautioned her sister. "There's someone in the hall now. I heard a step -"

There came a knock on the door, and in spite of themselves both girls started nervously.

"That isn't his rap!" whispered Alice.

"No. Ask who it is," suggested Ruth. Somehow, she looked

again to the younger Alice now.

"Who - who is it?" faltered the latter. "Maybe it's one of those horrid collectors," she went on, in her sister's ear. "I wish I'd kept quiet."

But the voice that answered reassured them.

"Are you there, Miss DeVere? This is Russ Dalwood. I want to apologize for that row outside your door a few minutes ago. It was an accident. I'm sorry. May I come in?"

CHAPTER III

THE OLD TROUBLE

For a moment the girls faced each other with wide-opened eyes, the brown ones of Alice gazing into the deep blue ones of Ruth. Ruth's eyes were not the ordinary blue - like those of a china doll. They were more like wood-violets, and in their depths could be read a liking for the unusual and romantic that was, in a measure, the key to her character. Not for nothing had Alice laughed at her sister's longing for a prince, on a milk-white steed, to come riding by. Ruth was tall, and of that desirable willowy type, so much in demand of late.

Alice was just saved from being a "bread-and-butter" girl. That is, she had wholesomeness, with a round face, and ruddy cheeks - more damask than red in color - but she also had a rollicking, good-natured disposition, without being in the least bit tomboyish. She reminded one of a girl just out of school, eager for a game of tennis or golf.

"Are you busy?" asked the voice on the other side of the door. "I can call again!"

"No, wait - Russ!" replied Ruth, with an obvious effort. "We had the chain on. We'll let you in!"

The DeVeres had only known their neighbors across the hall since coming to the Fenmore Apartment. Yet one could not live near motherly Mrs. Sarah Dalwood and not get to know her rather intimately, in a comparatively short time. She was what would have been called, in the country, "a good neighbor." In New York, with its hurry and scurry, where people live for years in adjoining rooms and never speak, she was an unusual type. She knew nearly every one in the big apartment - which was almost more than the janitor and his wife could boast.

A widow with two sons, Mrs. Dalwood was in fairly good circumstances - compared with her neighbors. Her husband had left her a little sum in life insurance that was well invested, and Russ held a place as moving picture machine operator in one of the largest of those theaters. He earned a good salary which made it unnecessary for his mother to go out to work, or to take any in, and his brother Billy was kept at school. Billy was twelve, a rather nervous, delicate lad, liked by everyone.

There was a rattle as the chain fell from the slotted slide on the door, and Alice opened the portal, to disclose the smiling and yet rather worried face of Russ. The girls had come to know him well enough to call him by his first name, and he did the same to them. It might not be out of place to say that Russ admired Ruth very much.

"I'm awfully sorry about what happened," began Russ. "You see I didn't mean to shove that fellow so hard. But he was awfully persistent, and I just lost my temper. I was afraid I'd shoved him downstairs."

"So were we," admitted Ruth, with a smile.

"Did he try to come in here, to escape from you?" asked Alice, with a frank laugh.

"Indeed he did not," replied Russ. "He caught at your door to save himself from falling. I guess he thought I was going to hit him; but I wasn't. I just shoved him away to keep him from coming back into our rooms again. Mother was a little afraid of him."

"Was he - was he a -" Alice balked at the word "collector."

"He was a fellow who's trying to steal a patent I'm working on!" exclaimed Russ, rather fiercely. "He's as unscrupulous as they come, and I didn't want him to get a foothold. So I just sent him about his business in a way I think he won't forget."

"Oh, are you working on a patent?" cried Ruth. "How nice! What's it about? Oh, I forgot! Perhaps you can't tell. It's a secret, I suppose. All patents are."

"Well, it isn't a secret from you folks," returned Russ. "I don't mind telling you, even though I haven't perfected it yet."

"Especially as you can be sure we girls wouldn't understand the least thing about it - if it has anything to do with machinery," put in Alice, laughing.

"Well, it is something about machinery," admitted Russ. "It is something new to go on moving picture machines, to steady the film as it moves behind the lens. You've often noticed how jerky the pictures are at times?" he asked.

"Yes; though we don't go very often," responded Ruth.

"Well, I've made a simple little device that fits on the machine. I needn't go into all details - to tell you the truth I haven't got 'em all worked out yet; but I think it will be a good thing, and bring me in some money.

"I've spoken to Mr. Frank Pertell, manager of the Comet Film Company, about it. I have done some work for him, you know. He says it will be a good thing, and, while it may not make me a millionaire, it will help a lot. So I'm working hard on it."

"But who was this man - what did he have to do with it?" asked Alice.

"He didn't have anything to do with it - but he wanted to. His name is Simpson Wolley - Simp, he's called for short, though he is not as simple as his name sounds. He heard about my invention - how, I don't know - and he's trying to get it away from me."

"Get it away from you?" echoed Alice.

"Yes. He came to me and wanted me to sell him the rights, just as it was, for a certain sum. I refused. Then to-day I came home unexpectedly. I found him in the room where I work, looking over my drawings and models. Mother had let him in to wait for me. She put him in the parlor, but he sneaked into my room. That's why I sent him flying."

"I don't blame you!" exclaimed Alice, with flashing eyes.

"Only I'm sorry he disturbed you," went on Russ. "I didn't mean to be quite so hasty; but he got on my nerves, I expect."

"Oh, that's all right," said Ruth, graciously.

"Mother said you might be frightened," went on the young man, "so she sent me here to tell you what it was."

"Don't mention it," laughed Alice. "We were a bit frightened at first, and we put the chain on the door. But are you sure you're all right - that he won't come back again?"

"Oh, you need not worry," Russ assured her. "He won't come here again; though I don't fancy I'm through with him. Simp Wolley hasn't much principle, and I know a lot of fellows who have done business with him to their sorrow. But he'll have to work hard to fool me. So my apology is accepted; is it?"

"Of course," laughed Ruth, blushing more than before.

Another step was heard in the hall.

"There's dad!" cried Alice. "Oh, where have you been?" she exclaimed, as she ran to her father's arms.

"I couldn't come sooner," the latter explained in his deep, mellow voice - a voice that had endeared him to many audiences. "We had to arrange about the rehearsals. Haven't you a kiss for dad, Ruth" he went on, putting his arms about the taller girl. "How are you, Russ?" and he nodded cordially. "Isn't it fine to have two such daughters as these?" He held them to him - one on either side.

"Father!" objected Ruth, blushing.

"Ha! Ashamed of her old daddy hugging and kissing her; is she?" Mr. DeVere laughed. "Well, I am surprised; aren't you, Russ? Some day -"

"Dad!" expostulated Ruth, blushing more vividly, and clapping a small hand over her father's mouth. "You mustn't say such things!"

"What things?" with a simulated look of innocent wonder.

"What you were going to say!"

"Well, as long as I didn't, no harm is done. What about lunch? I must go back this afternoon."

"I'll see you again," called Russ, retiring, for he knew father and daughters would want to exchange confidences.

"It's good news, Russ!" called Alice, as he departed across the hall. "Daddy has an engagement at last!"

"Glad to hear it, Mr. DeVere. I knew you'd land one sooner or later."

"Well, it came near being later, Russ, my boy."

"Now, Daddy dear, tell us all about it," begged Alice, when they were by themselves. "Isn't it just splendid! I wanted to get up a banquet, only there's nothing much on which to bank -"

"Alice, dear - such slang!" reproved Ruth.

"Never mind, better days are coming," said the actor. "At last I have a part just suited to me - one of the best for which I have ever been cast. It's with the 'A Matter of Friendship' company, and we open in about three weeks at the New Columbia. I feel sure I'll make a hit, and the play is a very good one - I may say a fine one."

"And you open in three weeks, you say, Dad?" asked Ruth, thoughtfully.

"Yes; or, rather, in two weeks from to-night. There are two weeks' rehearsals. But what - oh, I see. You mean there won't be any money coming in for three weeks - or until after the play has run a week. Well, never mind. I dare say we will manage somehow. I can likely get an advance on my salary. I'll see. And now for lunch. I'm as hungry as a stranded road company. What have you?"

"Not so very much," confessed Ruth. "I was hoping -"

There came a knock at the door.

"Come!" invited Mr. DeVere, and Russ appeared.

"Excuse this interruption," the young moving picture operator began, "but mother sent over to ask if you wouldn't take dinner with us. We have a big one. We expected my uncle and aunt, and they've disappointed us. Do come!"

Alice and Ruth looked at each other. Then they glanced up at their father, who regarded them thoughtfully.

"Well, I don't know," began the actor, slowly. "I - er -"

"Mother will be disappointed if you don't come," urged Russ. "She has chicken and biscuit for dinner, and she rather prides herself on it. The dinner will be spoiled if it isn't eaten hot - especially the biscuit, so she'll take it as a favor if you'll come over, and take the places of my uncle and aunt. Do come!" and he looked earnestly at Ruth.

"Well, what do you say, girls? Shall we accept of our neighbor's hospitality?" asked Mr. DeVere.

"Please do!" exclaimed Alice, in a tense whisper. "You know we haven't got a decent thing to eat in the ice box, and that delicatessen stuff -"

"Alice!" chided Ruth.

"Well, it's the truth!" insisted the merry girl, her brown eyes dancing with mischief. "Russ knows we aren't millionaires, and with papa out of an engagement so long - oh, chicken! Come on. I haven't tasted any in so long -"

"Alice - dear!" objected Ruth, sharply. "You mustn't mind her, Russ," she went on, rather embarrassed.

"I don't," he laughed. "But if you'll all come I'll promise you some of the best chicken you ever tasted. And mother's hot biscuits in the chicken gravy -"

"Don't you say another word, Russ Dalwood!" interrupted Alice. "We're coming!"

"I - I think we will," agreed Mr. DeVere, with a laugh.

Thus was his new engagement fittingly celebrated.

The memory of that chicken dinner lingered long with the DeVere family. For though there was daylight ahead there were dark and dreary days to be lived through.

As usual in theatrical companies, no salaries were paid while "A Matter of Friendship" was being rehearsed. Neither Mr. DeVere, nor any of the company, received any money for those two weeks of hard work. Those actors or actresses who had nothing put by lived as best they could on the charity of others. It was indeed "a matter of friendship" that some of them lived at all. And for a week after the play opened they could expect nothing. Then if the play should be a failure -

But no one liked to think of that.

The rehearsals went on, and the play was going to be a great success, according to Mr. DeVere. But then he always said that. What actor has not?

How he and his family lived those two weeks none but themselves knew. They had pawned all they dared, until their flat was quite bare of needed comforts. Tradesmen were insistent, and one man in particular threatened to have Mr. DeVere arrested if his bill was not paid. But it was out of the question to meet it. What little money was on hand was needed for food, and there was little enough of that.

Mr. DeVere did negotiate some small loans, but not enough to afford permanent relief. Perhaps motherly Mrs. Dalwood suspected, or Russ may have hinted at their neighbors' straits, for many a nourishing dish was sent to Ruth and Alice, on the plea that there was more of it than Mrs. Dalwood and her sons could eat.

There were more invitations from the Dalwoods to dinner or supper, but Mr. DeVere was proud, and declined, though in the most delightfully polite way.

"I - I don't see how he can refuse, when he knows we are really hungry!" sighed Alice.

"You wouldn't want him to be a beggar; would you?" flashed Ruth.

"No. But it's awfully hard; isn't it?"

"It is. Too bad they don't pay for rehearsals. And there'll be another full week! Oh, Alice, I wish there was something we could do to earn money!"

"So do I! But what is there?"

"I don't know. Oh, dear!"

They sat in the gloaming - silent, waiting for their father to come home.

"There's his step!" exclaimed Ruth, jumping up.

"Yes - but," said Alice, in puzzled, frightened tones, "it - it doesn't sound like him, somehow. How - how slowly he walks! Oh, I hope nothing has happened!"

"Happened? How could there?" asked Ruth, yet with blanched face.

The door opened, and Mr. DeVere entered. It needed but a glance at his white face to show that something had happened - something tragic - and not the tragedy of the theater.

"Oh, Father - Daddy - what is it!" cried Alice, springing to his arms.

"I - I - my -" Mr. DeVere could hardly speak, so hoarse was he. Only a husky whisper came from his lips.

"Are you - are you hurt?" cried Ruth. "Shall I get a doctor?"

"It - it's my voice!" gasped the actor. "It has gone back on me - I can't speak a word to be heard over the footlights! It's my old trouble come back!" and he sank weakly into a chair.

CHAPTER IV

DESPONDENCY

Startled and alarmed the two girls hastened to the side of their father. They flitted helplessly about him for a moment, like pretty, distressed birds. As for Mr. DeVere, his hand went to his aching throat as though to clutch the malady that had so suddenly gripped him, and tear it out. For none realized as keenly as he what the attack meant. It was as though some enemy had struck at his very life, for to him his voice was his only means of livelihood.

"Oh, Father!" gasped Ruth. "What is it? Speak! Tell us! What shall we do?"

"It - it's -" but his voice trailed off into a hoarse gurgle, and signs of distress and pain appeared on his face.

"Oh, tell us! Tell us!" begged Ruth, clasping her hands, her blue eyes filling with tears.

"Can't you see he can't speak!" exclaimed Alice, a bit sharply. She had a better grasp of the situation in this emergency than had her sister. "Something has happened to him! Was it dust in your throat on the street?" asked Alice. "Don't answer - wait, Dad! I have some lozenges. I'll get them for you!"

She was in and out of her room on the instant, with a box of troches, one of which she held out to her father. He had not moved since sinking into the chair, but stared straight ahead - and the future that he saw was not a pleasant one to contemplate.

"Take this, Father," begged Alice, slipping her arm about him, as she sank to the floor at his feet. "This will help your throat. Don't you remember what a terrible cold I had? These helped me a lot. Take one!"

Mr. DeVere shook his head slightly, and seemed about to refuse the lozenge. But a glance at his daughters' worried faces evidently made him change his mind. He slipped the tablet into his mouth, and then straightened up in his chair. Whatever happened to him he knew he must make a brave fight for the sake of the girls. It would not do to show the white feather before them, even though his heart was quaking with the terrible fear that had come upon him.

"What happened, Dad?" asked Ruth. "Can't you tell us? Oh, I am so worried!"

He tried to smile at her, but it was a pathetic attempt. Then, with an effort, he spoke - so hoarsely that they could barely understand him.

"It - it's my voice," he whispered, gratingly. "Some sort of affection of my vocal chords. You'd better get a doctor. I - I must be better by to-morrow."

"Poor Daddy!" whispered Ruth. "I'll go down stairs and telephone for Dr. Haldon."

"No - not him - some - some other physician. We - we haven't paid Dr. Haldon's bill," said Mr. DeVere quickly, and this time he spoke more distinctly.

"Oh, you're better!" cried Alice in delight, clapping her hands. "I knew my medicine would help you, Dad! It's good; isn't it?"

He nodded and smiled at her, but there was little of conviction in his manner, had the girls but noticed it.

"I know just how it is," went on Alice, and her tone did as much as anything to relieve the strain they were all under. "I caught cold once, and I got hoarse so suddenly that I was afraid I was going to be terribly ill. But it passed off in a day or two. Yours will, Dad!"

Mr. DeVere tried to act as though he believed it, but there was a despondent look on his face.

"I'll slip over and ask Mrs. Dalwood the name of a good doctor," offered Alice. "It's too bad we can't pay Dr. Haldon, but we will as soon as we can. Mrs. Dalwood may know of a good throat specialist nearby."

"Yes, you had better go," said Mr. DeVere in a low voice. "I must be able to go on with the rehearsals to-morrow."

Alice fairly flew across the hall, and the tragic little story was soon told. Mrs. Dalwood, fortunately, did know of a good doctor in the vicinity. He had attended Billy several times, and, while not exactly a throat specialist, was to be depended upon.

"Then I'll go downstairs and telephone for him," said Alice. "Poor daddy is so worried."

"I'll go over and see what I can do," volunteered Mrs. Dalwood. "I have an old-fashioned cough medicine I used for the children."

She took a bottle with her as she slipped across the hall to the flat of her neighbors. Russ went with her, anxious to do what he could.

But Mr. DeVere shook his head as the bottle of simple home remedy was proffered.

"Thank you very much, Mrs. Dalwood," he said hoarsely. "It is very kind of you, but I'm afraid to try it. I have had this trouble before, and -"

"You have, Father?" cried Ruth in surprise. "You never told us about it."

"I will - after the doctor comes," he said in a low voice.

Alice came back from using the telephone of the neighbor on the floor below to say that Dr. Rathby would soon be over.

"And then we'll have you all right again, Daddy!" she said, and the merry, laughing light that had disappeared came back into her eyes.

It was rather anxious waiting for the physician, but when he came his cheery, breezy presence seemed to fill them all with hope. He took Mr. DeVere into a room by himself, and made a careful examination. The girls could hear the young doctor's sharp, quick questioning, and their father's hoarse, mumbled replies. Then followed a period of nervous silence, broken by more talk.

Presently physician and patient came out Dr. Rathby looked serious, but he tried to smile. Mr. DeVere looked serious - but he did not smile. That was the difference.

"Well?" asked Ruth, with a sharp intaking of her breath.

"Nothing serious - at least, so far," was the doctor's verdict. "I think we have taken it in time. There is considerable inflammation of the vocal chords, and they have suffered a partial paralysis."

"As bad as that?" gasped Alice.

"Oh, that isn't half as bad as it sounds!" laughed Dr. Rathby. "I have had cases worse than this. Now, I'll leave you some medicine to be used in an atomizer, as a spray, Mr. DeVere, and I want you - in fact as a doctor I order you - to speak as little as possible. Don't use your voice at all, if you can help it - at least not for several days."

He turned to write a prescription, but was startled at the hoarse cry of expostulation from Mr. DeVere.

"But, doctor!" exclaimed the actor, "I - I -"

"There, now, I told you not to speak!" chided the physician, with upraised finger.

"But I have to! I'm an actor - I'm rehearsing a new part. I must use my voice! It's imperative!"

The doctor seemed startled.

"An actor," he said in low tones. "You did not tell me that. I did not understand ... Hm! Yes!"

He thought deeply for a moment.

"You could not take a rest for a week?" he asked.

"A week? No! I have been 'resting' enough weeks as it is. I must go on with this. I've had it before. It has passed away. Can't you give me something that will enable me to go on - some medicine that will act quickly? I must be at rehearsal to-morrow."

The doctor shrugged his shoulders as though to clear himself from all blame.

"Well, if you have to - you have to, I suppose," he said. "I understand. I can give you an astringent mixture that will shrink the chords, and may relieve some of the inflammation. It may enable you to go on - but at the risk of permanent injury to your throat."

"Oh!" exclaimed both girls.

"Never mind!" responded Mr. DeVere, hoarsely. "I - I must risk the future for the sake of the present. I cannot give up this engagement. I must keep on with the rehearsals. Give me something speedy, if you please, Doctor. I'll - I'll have to take the chance."

"I am sorry," spoke Dr. Rathby. "But of course I understand. I have a mixture that some singers have used with good effect. I'll try it on you. You can use it several times to-night, and on your way to rehearsal stop in at my office in the morning, and I'll swab out your throat. That may help some."

"Oh, thank you, Doctor. You don't know what this means to me. I - I feel better already."

"I'm afraid it's only temporary relief," returned the physician. "But there. Don't worry. Get that filled and see what effect it has. Then come and see me in the morning."

He wrote the prescription and hurried away, nodding to the girls.

"I'll get it filled," offered Ruth, and she could hardly keep back a sigh as she looked at the scanty supply of money in the household purse. As she was going out to the drug store she met Russ in the hallway.

"Is he any better?" the young moving picture operator asked.

"I think so," answered Ruth. "But isn't it too bad? Just when everything looked so bright."

"Oh, well, it will come out all right, I'm sure," spoke Russ. "Don't you want to come to see our show to-night? We've got some fine pictures. I'm going down a little early to get the reels in shape."

"We very seldom go to the 'movies,'" answered Ruth. "Though I have seen some I liked."

"We have some fine ones," went on Russ.

"Better come on down. I'll get you a pass in!" and he laughed genially.

"Not this time," answered Ruth gently. "I must get back and help Alice look after my father. Thank you."

She left him at the corner, and he passed on whistling softly and thinking of many things.

Mr. DeVere seemed better when Ruth got back with the medicine. And when his throat was sprayed he could talk with less effort. But his tones were still very husky, and it was evident that unless there was a great improvement in the morning he would hardly be able to go to rehearsal.

"I'm glad the show doesn't open until next week," he said with a smile. "I'd never be able to make myself heard beyond the first three rows. But I'll surely be better by the time we open."

"What did you mean by saying you had this same trouble before, Dad?" asked Alice.

"Well, it did come on me last summer, when I was taking my little vacation," he replied. "It wasn't quite as bad as this, though."

"You never told us," accused Ruth.

"No, I didn't want to worry you. It passed over, and I'm sure this will."

Mr. DeVere spoke little the next morning. Perhaps he did not want his daughters to know how very hoarse his voice was. He left for the doctor's before going to the theater, and most anxiously did the girls await his return.

"There he is!" exclaimed Ruth at length, late that afternoon.

"But he's earlier than usual!" said Alice. "I wonder -"

Mr. DeVere fairly staggered into the room. His face was white as he sank into a chair Alice pushed forward.

"Daddy!" exclaimed the girls.

He shook his head mournfully.

"It - it's no use!" he said, and they could barely make out his words. "My voice failed completely. I - I had to give up the rehearsal," and he covered his face with his hands.

CHAPTER V

REPLACED

For a few moments the two girls said nothing. They simply stood there, looking at their father, who was bowed with grief. It was something new for him - a strange role, for usually he was so jolly and happy - going about reciting odd snatches from the plays in which he had taken part.

"Does - does it hurt you, Daddy?" asked Ruth softly, as she stepped closer to him, and put her hand on his shoulder.

He raised himself with an effort, and seemed to shake off the gloom that held him prisoner.

"No - no," he answered in queer, croaking tones, so different from his usual deep and vibrant ones. "That's the odd part of it. I have no real pain. It isn't sore at all - just a sort of numbness."

"Did it come on suddenly?" asked Alice.

"Well, it did yesterday - very suddenly. But this time I was hoarse when I started to rehearse and it kept getting worse until I couldn't be heard ten feet away. Of course it was no use to go on then, so the stage manager called me off."

"Then he'll wait until you're better?" asked Alice.

Her father shrugged his shoulders.

"He'll wait until to-morrow, at any rate," was the hesitating answer.

"Didn't going to the doctor's office help any?" asked Ruth.

"For a few minutes - yes. But as soon as I got to the theater I was as bad as ever. I had some of his spray with me, too, but it did little good. I think I must see him again. I'll go to his office now."

"No, he must come here!" insisted Ruth. "You shouldn't take any chances going out in the air, Father, even though it is a warm spring day. Let him come here. I'll go telephone."

She was out into the hall before he could remonstrate, had he had the energy to do it. But Mr. DeVere seemed incapable of thinking for himself, now that this trouble had come upon him.

Dr. Rathby came a little later. He had a cheery, confident air that was good for the mind, if not for the body.

"Well, how goes it?" he asked.

"Not - very well," was Mr. DeVere's hoarse reply.

"I'm afraid you'll have to do as I suggested and take a complete rest," went on the doctor. "That's the only thing for these cases. I'll take another look at you."

The examination of the throat was soon over.

"Hum!" mused the physician. "Well, Mr. DeVere, I can tell you one thing. If you keep on talking and rehearsing, you won't have any voice at all by the end of the week."

"Oh!" cried the girls, together.

"Now, don't be frightened," went on the doctor quickly, seeing their alarm. "This may not be at all serious. There is a good chance of Mr. DeVere getting his voice back; but I confess I see little hope of it at the present time. At any rate he must give himself absolute rest, and not use his voice - even to talk to you girls," and he smiled at them.

"I know that is going to be hard," the doctor went on; "but it must be done sir, it must be done."

"Impossible!" murmured Mr. DeVere. "It cannot be!"

"It must be, my dear sir. Your vocal chords are in such shape that the least additional strain may permanently injure them. As it is now - you have a chance."

"Only a chance did you say?" asked the actor, eagerly.

"Yes, only a chance. It would be cruel to deceive you, and try to tell you that this is only temporary, and will pass off. It may, but it is sure to come back again, unless you give your throat an absolute rest."

"For - for how long?"

"I can't say - six months - maybe a year - maybe -"

"A year! Why, Doctor, I never could do that."

"You may have to. You can speak now, but if you keep on you will get to the point where you will be next to absolutely dumb!"

The girls caught their breaths in sharp gasps. Even Mr. DeVere seemed unnerved.

"It may seem harsh to say this to you," went on Dr. Rathby, "but it is the kindest in the end. Rest is what you need."

"Then I can't go to rehearsal in the morning?"

"Certainly not. I must forbid it as your physician. Can't you get a few days off?"

Mr. DeVere shook his head.

"Aren't there such things as understudies? Seems to me I have heard of them," persisted the physician.

"I - I wouldn't like to have to put one on," said the actor.

His daughters knew the reason. Times were but little better than they had been in the theatrical business. Many good men and women, too, were out of engagements, and every available part was quickly snapped up. Mr. DeVere had waited long enough for this opening, and now to have to put on an understudy when the play was on the eve of opening, might mean the loss of his chances. Theatrical managers were uncertain at best, and an actor in an important part, with a voice that would not carry beyond the first few rows, was out of the question.

Mr. DeVere knew this as well as did his daughters.

"I'll tell you what I'll do," went on Dr. Rathby. "I'll speak to your manager myself. I'll explain how things are, and say it is imperative that you have one or two days of rest. It may be that your chords will clear up enough in that time so that I can treat them better and you can resume your duties."

"Will you do that?" cried the actor, eagerly. "It will be awfully good of you. Just say to Mr. Gans Cross - he's the manager of the New Columbia theater - that I will be back in two days - less, if you will allow me, Doctor."

The physician shook his head.

"It must be at least two days," he said, and he went off to

telephone, promising to come back as soon as he could.

He did return, later in the evening, with a new remedy of which he said he had heard from a fellow doctor.

"What did Mr. Cross say?" Mr. DeVere asked eagerly.

"I have good news for you. He agreed to use an understudy for two days. He said you were letter-perfect in the part, anyway, and it was the others who really needed the rehearsing. So now we have two full days in which to do our best. And in that time I want you to talk the deaf and dumb language," laughed Dr. Rathby.

Mr. DeVere eagerly promised.

Then began a two-days' warfare against the throat ailment. Ruth and Alice were untiring in attendance on their father. They saw to it that he used the medicine faithfully, and they even got pads and pencils that he might write messages to them instead of speaking.

On his part the actor was faithful. He did not use his voice at all, and on the second day Dr. Rathby said there was some improvement. He was not very enthusiastic, however, and when Mr. DeVere asked if he could attend rehearsals next day the doctor said:

"Well, it's a risk, but I know how you feel about it. You may try it; but, frankly, I am fearful of the outcome."

"I - I've got to try," whispered Mr. DeVere.

He went to the rehearsal, and the worst fears of the physician were realized. After the first act Mr. DeVere was hoarser than ever before. The other players could not hear him to get their "cues," or signals when to reply, and come on the stage. The rehearsal had to be stopped. There was a hasty conference between the manager of the company and the treasurer of the same.

"The play will have to open on time," said the manager.

"Yes, we've had a big advance sale," replied the treasurer.

"And DeVere can't do it."

"No. I'll have to put his understudy in until we can cast someone else. I'll tell him."

The actor must have guessed what was coming, for he was washing off his make-up in the dressing-room when the manager entered.

"I'm awfully sorry about this, DeVere," began Mr. Cross. "But I'm afraid you won't be able to go on Monday night."

"No, Mr. Cross, I myself am of the same opinion. My voice has failed me utterly."

"And yet - and yet - you understand how it is. We must open on time."

"Yes, I know. The show must go on - the show must go on."'

"And the only way -"

"Is to replace me. I know. You can't help it, Mr. Cross. I know just how it is. It isn't your fault - it's my misfortune. I thank you for your patience. You'll have to - to replace me. It's the only thing to do. And yet," he added so softly that the manager did not hear "what am I to do? What are my daughters to do?"

CHAPTER VI

A NEW PROPOSITION

There was no need for Ruth and Alice to ask their father what had happened. One look at his ashen face when he came home from the theater was enough.

"Oh, Daddy!" cried Alice. "Couldn't you make it go?"

He answered with a shake of the head. The strain of the rehearsal had pained him.

"Did - did they put in someone else?" asked Ruth.

"Yes, I'm out of it for good - at least for this engagement."

"The mean things!" burst out Alice "I think that Mr. Cross is rightly named. I wish I could tell him so, too!"

"Alice!" reproved Ruth, gently.

"I don't care!" cried the younger girl, her brown eyes sparkling. "The idea of not waiting a few days with their show until papa was better; and he the leading man, too."

"They couldn't wait, Alice, my dear," explained Mr. DeVere. "Cross did all he could for me, and allowed me two days. But it is out of the question. Dr. Rathby was right. I need a long rest - and I guess I'll have to take it whether I want to or not."

Then, seeing the anxious looks on the faces of his daughters, he went on, in more cheerful, though in no less husky tones:

"Now don't worry, girls. There'll be some way out of this. If I can't act I can do something else. I'm well and strong, for which I must be thankful. I'm not ill and, aside from my voice, nothing is the matter. I'll look for a place doing something else beside stage work, until my voice is restored. Then I'll take up my profession again. Come, there is nothing to worry about."

There was - a-plenty; but he chose to ignore it for the time being. He knew, as well as did the girls, that there was little money left, and that pressing bills must soon be met. Added to them, now, would be one from the physician and Mr. DeVere would need more medical attention.

"I'm going to start out, the first thing in the morning, and look for a place," went on the actor.

"Oh, but you must be careful of your voice," said Alice. "If you don't you may harm it permanently."

"Oh I'll be careful," her father promised. "I'll take along a pad and pencil, and pretend to be dumb. But I'll speak if it's absolutely necessary. Now that there is no particular object in holding myself for the place in 'A Matter of Friendship,' and with the strain of rehearsal over, I won't be so afraid of talking. Yes, in the morning I'll start out."

"I wish we could start out," said Alice to Ruth in the latter's room, later that night. "Why can't we do something to earn money?"

"We may have to - if it comes to that," agreed Ruth. "There are some bills that must be paid or -"

"Or what, Sister?"

"Never mind, don't you worry. Perhaps it will come out all

right, after all. Father may get a place. He knows many persons in the theatrical business, and if he can't get behind the footlights he may get a place in front - in the box office, or something like that."

"Fancy poor father, with all his talents as an actor, taking tickets, though!"

"Well, it will be a humiliation, of course," agreed Ruth. "But what can be done? We have to live."

"Oh, if only I were a boy!" cried Alice, with a flash of her brown eyes. "I'd do something then!"

"What would you do?" asked Ruth.

"I - I'd turn the crank of a moving picture machine if I couldn't get anything else to do. Look at Russ - he earns good money at the business."

"Yes, I know. But we can't be boys, Alice."

"No - more's the pity. But I'm going to do something!"

"What, Alice? Nothing rash, I hope," said the older sister, quickly. "You know father -"

"Oh, don't worry. I won't cause any sensation. But I'm going to do something. There's no use in two strong, healthy girls sitting around, and letting poor old daddy, with a voice like a crow's, doing all the work and worrying."

"No, I agree with you, and if there is anything I could do I'd do it."

"That's it!" exclaimed Alice, petulantly. "Girls ought to be brought up able to do something so they could earn their living if they had to, instead of sitting around doing embroidery or tinkling on the piano. I wouldn't know even how to clerk in a store if I had to."

"I hope you won't have to, Alice."

"So do I. I shouldn't like it, but there are worse things than that. I know what I am going to do, though."

"What?"

"I'm going to look through the advertisements in the paper to-morrow, and start out after the most promising places."

"Oh, Alice!"

"Well, what else is there to be done?" asked the younger girl, fiercely. "We've got to live. We've got to have a place to stay, and we've got to pay the bills that are piling up. Can you think of anything else to do?"

"No, but something may - turn up."

"I'm not going to wait for it. I'm not like Mr. Micawber. I'm going out and turn up something for myself. There's one thing I can do, and that's manicure. I could get a place at that, maybe," and Alice looked at her pretty and well-kept nails, while Ruth glanced at her own hands.

"Yes, dear, you do that nicely. But isn't it - er - rather common?"

"All work is 'common,' I suppose. It's also common to starve - but I'm not going to do it if I can help it. Good-night!" and she flounced into her own room.

"Oh, dear!" sighed Ruth. "I wish Alice were not so - so lively" and she cried softly before she fell asleep.

Mr. DeVere was up early the next morning. He seemed more cheerful, though his voice, if anything, was hoarser and more husky than ever.

"Here's where I start out to seek my fortune!" he said raspingly, though cheerfully, after a rather scanty breakfast. "I'll come back with good news - never fear!"

He kissed the girls good-bye, and went off with a gay wave of his hand.

"Brave daddy!" murmured Ruth.

"Yes, he is brave," said Alice "and we've got to be brave, too."

"Where are you going?" asked Ruth, as she saw her sister dressing for the street.

"Out."

"Out where? I must know."

"Well, if you must, I'm going to make the rounds of the manicuring parlors."

"Oh, Alice, I hate to have you do it. Some of those places where men go -"

"I'm only going to apply at the ladies' parlors."

"Oh, well, I - I suppose it's the only thing to do."

"And if worse comes to worst!" cried Alice, gaily, "I'll get some orange-sticks and we'll stew them for soup. It can't be much worse than boot-leg consomme."

"Oh, Alice!" cried Ruth. "You are hopeless."

"Hopeless - but not - helpless! *Auf Wiedersehen!*"

But in spite of her gay laugh as she closed the hall door after her, Alice DeVere's face wore a look of despondency. She knew how little chance she stood in New York - in big New York.

And perhaps it was this despondent look that caused Russ Dalwood to utter an exclamation as he met her down at the street door of the apartment house.

"What's the matter?" Alice replied to his startled ejaculation. "Is my hat on crooked; or did one of my feathers get into your eye? Foolish styles; aren't they?"

"No - nothing like that; only you looked - say, Alice, has anything happened?"

"Yes, Russ, there is something the matter," replied Alice, frankly. "Do you know of anybody who wants a young lady to do anything - that a young lady, such as I, could do?"

He laughed.

"I'm serious," she said, and a glance at her pretty face confirmed this. There was a resolute look in her brown eyes.

"Are you looking for work?" Russ asked.

"I am. I was thinking of trying to be a manicurist -"

He made a gesture of disapproval.

"Well, what can I do? I must do something. Poor daddy's voice has failed utterly. He can't take his new part in the play unless he does it in pantomime, and I'm afraid that would hardly be the thing. He simply can't speak his lines, though he can act them."

"That's too bad," said Russ, sympathetically.

"So they had to get another actor in his place," went on Alice, "and poor father has started out to look for something else to do. That's my errand this morning, also."

Russ was in deep thought for a moment. Then he exclaimed:

"I have it!"

"What? A place for me?" demanded Alice. "Tell me at once, and I'll hurry there."

"No, Alice, not a place for you; but a place for your father. You say he can't speak, but he can act?"

"Yes."

"Then the movies is the very place for him! He won't have to say a word - just move his lips. He can act parts in photoplays as well as if he never had a voice. I just thought of it. It will be the very thing he can do. Say, I'm glad I met you. We must get busy with this at once.

"Come on! I'm on my way now to see about my new patent, and I can take you to the manager of the film company. I know him well. I'm sure he'll give your father a place in the company, and it pays well. If Mr. DeVere can't act at the New Columbia he can in the movies! Come on!"

CHAPTER VII

ALICE CHANGES HER MIND

Filled with enthusiasm over his new project for aiding Mr. DeVere, Russ Dalwood caught Alice by the hand, and guided her steps with his. She had been about to turn off at a corner, to carry out her intention of seeking employment in one of the many manicure parlors on a certain street. Now she hesitated.

"Well," asked Russ, impatiently, "don't you like the idea?"

"Oh, it's fine - it's splendid of you!" Alice replied, with fervor, "but you know -"

She hesitated, her cheeks taking on a more ruddy hue. There was an uncertain look in her brown eyes.

"Well, what?" asked Russ, smilingly. "Surely you don't mind going with me to the manager's office? It's a public place. Lots of girls go there, looking for engagements."

"Oh, no, it isn't that!" she hastened to assure him.

"Or, if you don't like going with me, I can give you a note to Mr. Pertell, the manager. I know him quite well, as I've been negotiating with him about my patent."

"Oh, Russ, you know it isn't that!" she exclaimed.

"And, if you like, we'll go back and get Ruth. Maybe that would be better!" he exclaimed eagerly, and as Alice looked into his honest gray eyes she read his little secret, and smiled at him understandingly.

"Oh, never that!" she cried gaily. "Ruth would be the last one in the world to be let into this secret, until it is more assured of success. Besides, I guess when you walk with Ruth you don't want me," she challenged.

"Oh, now -" he began.

"That's all right. I understand," she laughed at him. "No, we won't tell Ruth."

"Then you'll go and see the manager - I know he'll give your father a trial, and that's all that's needed, for I'm sure he can do the acting. And they're always looking for new characters. Come on!"

Once more, in his enthusiasm, he tried to lead her down the street. But she hung back.

"No, really, Russ," she said earnestly enough now, and her eyes took on a more grave and serious look. "It isn't that. It's only - well, I might as well tell you, though it may be rather mean after your kindness. But my father thinks the movies are so - so vulgar! There - I've said it."

She looked at her companion anxiously. To her surprise Russ laughed.

"So, you were afraid of hurting my feelings; were you?" he asked.

"Yes," she answered, in a low voice.

"Nothing like that!" he assured her. "I've heard worse things than that said about the movies. But I want to tell you that you're wrong, and, with all due respect to him, your father is wrong too. There's nothing vulgar or low about the movies - except the price."

He was becoming really enthusiastic now. His voice rang, and his eyes sparkled.

"I'm not saying that because I make my living at them, either," Russ went on. "It's because it's true. The moving picture shows were once, perhaps, places where nice persons didn't go. But it's different now. All that has been changed. Why, look at Sarah Bernhardt, doing her famous plays before the camera? Even Andrew Carnegie consented to give one of his speeches in front of the camera, with a phonograph attachment, the other day."

"Did he, really?" cried Alice.

"He certainly did. And a lot of the best actors and actresses in this and other countries aren't ashamed to be seen in the movies. They're glad to do it, and glad to get the money, too, I guess," he added, with a grin.

"I think it would be the very thing for your father. Of course, if his voice had held out he might like it better to be an actor on the real stage. But in the movies he won't have to talk. He'll just have to act. Then, when his voice gets better, as I hope it will, he can take up the legitimate again."

"Oh, I know his heart is set on that!" exclaimed Alice.

"But don't you think he'd consider this?" asked Russ. He was very anxious to help - Alice could tell that.

"I - I'm afraid he wouldn't," confessed the girl. "He thinks the movies too common. I know, for I've heard him say so many times."

"They're not common!" defended Russ, sturdily. "The moving

pictures are getting better and better all the while. Of course some poor films are shown, but they're gradually being done away with. The board of censorship is becoming more strict.

"Common! Why do you know that it costs as much as $20,000, sometimes, to stage one of the big plays - one with lots of outdoor scenes in it, burning buildings, railroad accidents made to order, and all that."

"Really?" cried Alice, her eyes now shining with excitement.

"That's right!" exclaimed Russ. "I'm just at the beginning of the business. I've learned the projecting end of it so far. Almost anyone can put the film in the machine, switch on the light, get the right focus and turn the handle. But it's harder to film a real drama with lots of excitement in it - outdoor stuff - cattle stampeded - the sports of cowboys - a fake Indian fight; it takes lots of grit to stand up in front of an oncoming troop of horsemen, and snap them until they get so close you can see the whites of their eyes. Then if they turn at the right time - well and good. But if there's a slip, and they ride into you - good-night! Excuse my slang," he added, hastily.

"Did that ever happen?" she asked, eagerly.

"Well, if not that, something near enough like it. I've heard the operators - those who take the negatives - tell of 'em many a time. That's what I'm going to be soon - a taker of the moving picture plays instead of just projecting them on the screen. Mr. Pertell has promised to give me a chance. He's organizing some new companies.

"Just as soon as I get my patent perfected he's promised to put it on his machines. Then I'm going with his company."

"Did you hear any more about that man you say tried to steal your invention?" asked Alice.

"Who, Simp Wolley? Oh, yes, he's been sneaking around after

me, and I told him what I thought of him. He's got another fellow in with him - Bud Brisket - and he's about the same type. But I'm not going to worry about it."

"Don't be too confident," warned Alice. "I've heard of many inventors whose patents were gotten away from them."

"Thanks, I'll be careful. But just now I'm interested in getting your father to take up this work. I know he'll like it, once he tries it. Won't you come and see the manager? I'm sure he'll give your father a trial."

Alice stood in deep thought for a moment. Then with a little gesture, as though putting the past behind her, she exclaimed:

"Yes, Russ, I will, and I thank you! I told Ruth I was going to do something, and I am. If father can get an engagement I won't have to go to work. Not that I'm ashamed to work - I love it!" she added hastily. "But I wouldn't like to be a public manicurist, and that's the only situation that seemed open to me. I will go see your manager, Russ, and I'll do my best to get father to take up this work. It's quite different from what I thought it was."

"I knew you'd say that," chuckled Russ. "Come on."

"What would Ruth say if she saw me now?" Alice asked, as she and Russ walked off together. "She would certainly think I was defying all conventionality."

"Don't worry." Russ advised her. "It's the sensible thing to do. And I'll explain to Ruth, too."

"Oh, I believe you could explain to anyone!" Alice declared with enthusiasm. "You've made it so clear and different to me. But how do they make moving pictures?"

"You'll soon see," he answered. "We're going to one of the film studios now. This is about the time they begin to make the scenes. It's very interesting."

Soon they found themselves before a rather bare brick building. It had nothing of the look of a theater about it. There were no gaudy lithographs out in front, no big frames with the pictures of the actors and actresses, or of scenes from the plays. There was no box office - no tiled foyer. It might have been a factory. Alice's face must have shown the surprise she felt, for Russ said:

"This is where the films are made. It's all business here. They make the inside scenes here - anything from the interior of a miner's shack to a ballroom in a king's palace. Of course, for outside scenes they go wherever the scenery best suits the story of the play. And here the film negatives are developed, and duplicate positives made for the projecting machines. This is Mr. Pertell's principal factory."

"Fancy a play-factory!" exclaimed Alice.

"That's exactly what it is - a play-factory," agreed Russ. "Come on in."

If Alice was surprised at the exterior appearance of the building the interior was more bewildering. They passed rapidly through the departments devoted to the mechanical end of the business - where the films were developed and printed. Russ promised to show her more of that later.

"We'll go right up to the theatre studio," he said.

Alice looked about the big room, that seemed filled with all sorts of scenery, parts of buildings, rustic bridges - in short, all sorts of "props." She had been behind the scenes often in some of the plays in which her father took part, so this was not startlingly new to her. Yet it was different from the usual theatre.

And such strange "business" seemed going on. There were men

and women going through plays - Alice could tell that, but the odd part of it was that in one section of the room what seemed a tragedy in a mountain log cabin was being enacted; while, not ten feet away, was a parlor scene, showing men in evening dress, and women in ball costumes, gliding through the mazes of a waltz. Next to this was a scene representing a counterfeiter's den in some low cellar, with the police breaking through the door with drawn revolvers, to capture the criminals.

And in front of these varied scenes stood a battery of queer cameras - moving picture cameras, looking like flat fig boxes with a tube sticking out, and a handle on one side, at which earnest-faced young men were vigorously clicking.

And, off to one side, stood several men in their shirt sleeves superintending the performances. They gave many directions.

"No, not that way! When you faint, fall good and hard, Miss Pennington!"

"Hurry now, Mr. Switzer; get in some of that funny business! Look funny; don't act as though this was your funeral!"

"Come on there Mr. Bunn; this isn't 'Hamlet.' You needn't stalk about that way. There's no grave in this!"

"Hold on, there! Cut that part out. Stop the camera; that will have to be done over. There's no life in it!"

And so it went on, in the glaring light that filtered in through the roof, composed wholly of skylights, while a battery of arc lamps, in addition, on some of the scenes, poured out their hissing glare to make the taking of the negatives more certain.

Alice was enthralled by it all. She stood close to Russ's side, clasping his arm. Many of the men engaged in taking the pictures knew the young operator, and nodded to him in friendly fashion, as they hurried about. Some of the actors and actresses, too, bowed to the young fellow and smiled. He seemed a general favorite.

"Isn't it wonderful?" whispered Alice. "I had no idea the making of a moving picture was anything like this!"

"I thought you'd change your mind," replied Russ, with a laugh. "But you haven't seen half of it yet. Here comes Mr. Pertell now. I'll speak to him about your father."

CHAPTER VIII

"PAY YOUR RENT, OR -"

Alice liked the appearance of Mr. Pertell, manager of the Comet Film Company, from her first glimpse of him. He seemed so sturdy, kind and wholesome. He was in his shirt sleeves, and his clothing was in almost as much disorder as his ruffled hair. But there was a kindly gleam in his snapping eyes, and a firm look about his mouth that showed his character.

"Oh, Mr. Pertell, can you spare a moment?" Russ called to him.

"Oh, hello, Russ; is that you?" was the cordial greeting. "How is the patent? I could use it if I had it now. Spare a minute? Yes, several of 'em. They've spoiled that one act and it's got to be done over. I don't see why they can't do as they're told instead of injecting a lot of new business into the thing! I've got to sit still and do nothing now for ten minutes while they fix that scene up over again. Go ahead, Russ - what can I do for you?"

He sat down on an overturned box, and motioned for Russ and Alice to occupy adjoining ones. Clearly there was not much ceremony about this manager. He was like others Alice had observed behind the scenes in real theatres, except that he did not appear so irascible.

"This is Miss Alice DeVere," began Russ, "and she has come to you about her father. He has lost his voice, and she and I think he might fit in some of your productions, where you don't need any talking."

"Yes, sometimes the less talking in the movies the better," agreed Mr. Pertell. "But you do need acting. Can your father act, Miss?"

"He is Hosmer DeVere," broke in Russ. "He was with the New Columbia Theatre Company. They were to open in 'A Matter of Friendship,' but Mr. DeVere's throat trouble made him give it up."

"Hosmer DeVere! Yes, I've heard of him, and I've seen him act. So he wants an engagement here; eh?"

"Oh, it isn't exactly that!" interrupted Alice, eagerly. "He - he doesn't know a thing about it yet."

"He doesn't know about it?" repeated the manager, wonderingly.

"No. He - I - Oh, perhaps you'd better tell him, Russ," she finished.

"I will," Russ agreed, with a smile. And, while Alice looked at some of the other dramas being enacted before the clicking eyes of the cameras, her companion told how it had been planned to overcome the prejudice of Mr. DeVere and get him to try his art with the "movies."

Alice was tremendously interested, and looked on with eager eyes as the actors and actresses enacted their roles. Some of them spoke, now and then, as their lines required it, for it has been found that often audiences can read the lips of the players on the screen. But there was no need for any loud talking - in fact, no need of any at all - whispering would have answered. Indeed some actors find that they can do better work without saying a word - merely using gestures. Others, who have long been identified with the legitimate drama, find it hard to break away from the habit of years and speak their lines aloud.

"Oh, I'm sure father would like this," thought Alice. "And he wouldn't have to use his poor throat at all. I must tell him all about it."

She looked at two girls - they did not seem much older than herself and Ruth, who were playing a scene in a "society" drama. They were both pretty, but Alice thought they were rather too flippant in manner when out of the scene. They laughed and joked with the other actors, and with the machine men.

But the latter were too busy focusing their cameras, and getting all that went on in the scenes, to pay much attention to anything else. The least slip meant the spoiling of many feet of film, and while this in itself was not so expensive, it often meant the making of a whole scene over again at a great cost.

"Well," Mr. Pertell said at length, "I am greatly interested in Mr. DeVere. I know him to be a good actor, and I greatly regret his affliction. I think I can use him in some of these plays. Can he ride a horse - does he know anything about cowboy life, or miners?" he asked Alice.

"Oh, I'm sure daddy wouldn't want to do any outdoor plays," the girl exclaimed. "He is so used to theatrical scenes."

"Well, I might keep him in "parlor" drama," Mr. Pertell remarked. "Please tell him to come and see me," he went on. "I would like to talk to him."

"Thank you, so much!" returned Alice, gratefully. "I shall tell him, and - well, there's no use saying I'm sure he'll come," she went on with a shrug of her shoulders. "It's going to be rather difficult to break this to him. It - it's so - different from what he has been used to."

"I can understand," responded Mr. Pertell. "But I think if he understood he would like it. Tell him to come here and see how we do things."

"I will!" Alice promised.

Russ escorted her to the street, and then, as he had to see about some changes in the working of his proposed patent, he bade her good-bye. She said she would find her way home all right.

"Well?" asked Ruth, as Alice entered the apartment a little later, "did you do anything rash?"

"Perhaps!" Alice admitted, as she took off her hat, jabbed the pins in it and tossed it to one chair, while she sank into another.

"Oh, Alice! You - aren't going to be one of those - manicures; are you?"

"I hope not, though there are lots worse things. A manicure can be just as much a lady as a typist. But, Ruth, I have such news for you! I have found an engagement for dad!"

"An engagement for daddy?"

"Yes. In the movies! Listen. Oh, it was so exciting!"

Then, with many digressions, and in rather piece-meal manner, interrupting herself often to go back and emphasize some point she had forgotten, Alice told of her morning trip with Russ. She enlarged on the manner in which the moving pictures were made, until Ruth grew quite excited.

"Oh, I wish I could see how it is done!" she cried.

"You may - when dad takes this engagement," said Alice.

"He never will," declared her sister. "You know what he thinks of the movies."

"But he thinks wrong!" exclaimed Alice. "It's so different from what I thought."

"He'll never consent," repeated Ruth. "Hark! Here he comes now. Perhaps he has found something to do."

Footsteps were heard coming along the hallway. Alice glanced at the table before which her sister was sitting.

"What are you doing?" she asked.

"Looking over our bills, and trying to make five dollars do the work of fifteen," answered Ruth, with a wry smile. "Money doesn't stretch well," she added.

Mr. DeVere came in. It needed but a look at his face to show that he had been unsuccessful, but Ruth could not forbear asking:

"Well, Daddy?"

"No good news," he answered, hoarsely. "I could hardly make myself understood, and there seem few places where one can labor without using one's voice. I never appreciated that before."

"But I have found a place!" cried Alice, with girlish enthusiasm. "I have a place for you Daddy, where you won't have to speak a word."

"Where - where is it?" he whispered, and they both noted his pitiful eagerness.

"In the movies!" Alice went on. "Oh, it's the nicest place! I've been there, and the manager -"

"Not another word!" exclaimed Mr. DeVere. "I never would

consent to acting in the moving pictures. I would not so debase my profession - a profession honored by Shakespeare. I never would consent to it. The movies! Never!"

There was a knock at the door.

"I'll see who it is," offered Ruth, with a sympathetic glance at Alice, who seemed distressed. Then, as Ruth saw who it was, she drew back. "Oh!" she exclaimed, helplessly.

"Who is it?" asked Mr. DeVere, rising.

"I've come for the rent!" exclaimed a rasping voice. "This is about the tenth time, I guess. Have you got it?" and a burly man thrust himself into the room from the hall.

"The rent - Oh!" murmured Mr. DeVere, helplessly. "Let me see; have we the rent ready, Ruth?"

"No," she answered, with a quick glance at the table where she had been going over the accounts, and where a little pile of bills lay. "No, we haven't the rent - to-day."

"And I didn't expect you'd have it," sneered the man. "But I've come to tell you this. It's either pay your rent or -" He paused significantly and nodded in the direction of the street.

"Three days more - this is the final notice," and thrusting a paper into the nerveless hand of Mr. DeVere, the collector strode out.

CHAPTER IX

MR. DEVERE DECIDES

Mr. DeVere sank into a chair. Ruth looked distressed as her father glanced over the dispossess notice, for such it was. But on the face of Alice there was a triumphant smile. For she saw that this was the very thing needed to arouse her father to action. Despite the distastefulness of the work, she felt sure he would come finally to like acting before the camera.

The collector's call had been very opportune, though it was embarrassing.

"This - this," said Mr. DeVere, haltingly - "this is very - er - very unfortunate. Then we are behind with the rent, Ruth?"

"Yes, Dad. You know I told you -"

"Yes, I suppose so," he added, with a sigh. "I had forgotten. There have been so many things -"

He was lost in thought for a moment.

"Do we owe much more, Ruth?" he asked.

"Quite some, Daddy. But don't worry. You are not well, and -"

"No, I am not well. I feel very poorly, but it is mainly mental, and not physical - except for my throat. And even that does not really hurt. It is only - only that I cannot speak."

His voice trailed off into a hoarse whisper, which the girls could barely distinguish.

"I - I must find something to do," went on the stricken actor. "I'll go out again this afternoon. Let us have a little lunch and I will try again. I'll do anything -"

"Then, Daddy, why don't you let me tell about the moving pictures?" broke in Alice. "I'm sure -"

"Alice, dear, you know that isn't in my line," replied her father. "It is very good of you to suggest it; but it will not do. I could not bring myself to it -"

He paused, and looked dejectedly at the dispossess notice in his hand.

"I - I could not do it," he added with a sigh. "I must try to get something in the line of my profession. Perhaps I might get a place in some dramatic school. I have trained you girls in the rudiments of acting, and I'm sure I could do it with a larger class. I did not think of it before. Get me some lunch, Ruth, and I'll go out again."

"But what about the rent?" asked Alice. "We can't be put out on the street, Dad."

"No, I suppose not. I'll see Mr. Cross, and get another loan. I'll pay him back out of my first salary. We must have a roof over us. Oh, girls, I am so sorry for you!"

"Don't worry about us, Daddy! You just get better and take care of your throat!" urged Alice. "You might try the movies, just for a little while, and then -"

"Never! Never!" he interrupted with vigor. "I could not think of it!"

Again there came a knock at the door.

"I'll go," offered Alice.

"No, let me," said Ruth, quickly.

She slipped out into the hall, and closed the door after her. There was a low murmur of voices, gradually growing louder on the part of the unseen caller. Ruth seemed pleading. Then Mr. DeVere and Alice heard:

"It's no use. The boss says he won't send around any more meat until the bill is paid. He told me to tell you he couldn't wait any longer - that's all there is to it!"

"Oh!" 'said Alice, in a low voice.

"What does that mean?" asked Mr. DeVere, from the reverie into which he had fallen.

"I think it means," replied Alice, with a laugh in which there was little mirth, "think it means that we won't have any meat for lunch, Dad."

"Bless my soul!" exclaimed the actor.

Ruth came in with flushed face.

"Who was it?" asked her father, though there was no need.

"Only the butcher's boy. He said -"

"We heard," interrupted Alice, significantly. "Have we any eggs?" she asked, grimly.

"This - this is positively too much!" said Mr. DeVere. "I shall tell that meat man -"

"I'm afraid he wouldn't listen to you, Daddy," interposed

Ruth, gently. "We do owe him quite a bill. I suppose we can't blame him," and she sighed.

"I - I'll go at once and see Mr. Cross, my former manager," exclaimed Mr. DeVere. "He will make me a loan, I'm sure. Then I'll pay this butcher bill, and tell the insulting fellow that we shall seek a new tradesman."

"Then there's the rent, Daddy," said Ruth, in a low voice.

"Oh, yes - the rent. I forgot about that." The dispossess notice rustled in his hand. "The rent - Oh, yes. That must be paid first. I - I will have to get a larger loan. Well, get me what lunch you can, Ruth, my dear, and I'll go out at once."

Alice did not say "movies" again, not even when the very modest and frugal lunch was set. And it was about the "slimmest" meal, from a housekeeper's standpoint, that had ever graced the DeVere table, used as they had become to scanty rations of late. Mr. DeVere said little, but he appeared to be doing considerable thinking and Alice allowed him to do it without interruption. She seemed to know how, and when, to hold her tongue.

When he had gone out Ruth and Alice talked matters over. First they counted up what money they had, and figured how far it would go. If they paid the rent they would not have enough to live on for a week, and food was almost as vital a necessity as was a place to stay. There were other pressing bills, in addition to those of the butcher and the landlord.

"Don't you see, Ruth, that daddy's going into the movies will be our only salvation?" asked Alice.

"It does seem so. Yet could he do it?"

"He could - if he would. I saw some very poor actors there to-day."

"But is the pay sufficient?"

"It is very good, Russ says. And it increases with the fame of the actor. I wish I could get into the movies myself."

"Alice DeVere!"

"I don't care; I do! It's just lovely, I think. You don't have to act before a whole big audience that is staring at you. Just some nice men, in their shirt sleeves, turning cranks -"

"In their shirt sleeves?"

"Why, yes. It's quite warm, with all those arc lights glowing, you know. And besides, what are shirt sleeves? Didn't dad act in his during the duel scene in "Lord Graham's Secret?" Of course he did! Shirt sleeves are no disgrace. Oh, Ruth, what are we to do, anyhow? What is to become of us?"

Alice put her head down on the table.

"There, dear, don't cry," urged her sister. "There must be a way out. Father will get a loan - his voice will come back, and -"

"It will be too late," replied Alice, in a low voice. "We will be put out - disgraced before all the neighbors! I can't stand it. I'm going to do something!"

She arose quickly, and there was a look on her face that caused Ruth to give start and to cry out:

"Alice! What do you mean?"

"I mean I'm going to see Russ Dalwood and ask him if I can't get work in the movies. If father won't, I will! And I'll ask Russ for the loan of some money. I can pay him back when I get my salary!"

"Alice, I'll never let you do that!" and Ruth planted herself before the door.

For a tense moment the sisters confronted each other.

"But we - we must do something," faltered Alice.

"Yes, but not that - at least, not yet. We have some pride left. Wait - wait until father comes back."

With a gesture Alice consented. She sank wearily into a chair.

It was tedious waiting. The girls talked but little - they had no heart for it. Around them hummed the noise of the apartment house. Noises came to them through the thin, cheap walls. The crying of babies, the quarrels of a couple in the flat back of them, the wheeze of a rusty phonograph, and the thump-thump of a playerpiano, operated with every violation of the musical code, added to the nerve-racking din.

Ruth made a gesture of despair.

"Beautiful!" murmured Alice as the paper roll in the mechanical piano got a "kink," and played a crash of discords. Ruth covered her ears with her hands.

There was a step in the corridor.

"There's father!" exclaimed Ruth.

"I wonder what success he had negotiating a loan?" observed Alice.

Mr. DeVere entered wearily.

The girls waited for him to speak, and it was with an obvious effort that he croaked:

"I - I didn't get it. Mr. Cross wouldn't even see me. He sent out word that he was too busy. He is getting ready for the first performance of 'A Matter of Friendship,' to-night."

"A matter of friendship," repeated Alice. "What a play on the words!"

"I sent in my card," explained Mr. DeVere, "and told him I must have a little money. He sent back word that he was sorry, but that he had invested so much in the play that he could spare none."

There was a period of silence. The girls looked pityingly at their father.

"Something must be done," he declared, finally. "I can try elsewhere. I will go see -"

A knock at the door interrupted him. Before Alice could speak Ruth had gained it. She tried to close it, but was not in time to prevent the caller from being heard.

"The boss says there's no use orderin' any more groceries, until youse has paid for what youse has got," said a coarse voice. "Take it from me - nothin' doin'!"

"Oh!" Ruth was heard to murmur.

Mr. DeVere started from his chair.

"The insulting -" he began.

Alice touched him on the arm.

"Don't!" she begged, softly.

Mr. DeVere turned aside. He slipped his arm around Alice, and, as Ruth came in, with tears in her eyes, she, too, found a haven in her father's embrace. Then the actor spoke.

"Alice, dear," he faltered, "What is the address of that - that moving picture manager?"

CHAPTER X

THE MAN IN THE KITCHEN

Let it be said of Alice that, even in this moment of triumph, she did not gloat over her victory - for victory it was. Had she planned it, events could not have transpired to better purpose. The combination of circumstances had forced her father along the line of least resistance into the very path she would had chosen for him, and she felt in her soul that it was best.

But she did not say: "There, I knew you'd come to it, Daddy!" Many a girl would, and so have spoiled matters. Alice merely looked demurely at her father - and gave him the address.

The girl was perhaps wiser than her years would indicate, and certainly in this matter she was more resourceful than was Ruth. But then chance had played into her hands. That meeting with Russ had done much.

"Yes, I think I must come to it," sighed Mr. DeVere. "It is being forced on me - the movies. I never thought I would descend to them!"

"It isn't a fall at all, Daddy!" declared Alice, stoutly. "I'm glad you are going into them. You'll like them, I'm sure."

"The actors - and actresses - if one can call them such - who take parts in moving picture plays must be very - very crude sort of persons," he said.

"Not at all!" cried Alice. "I was there and saw them, and there were some as nice as you'd want to meet. They were real gentlemen and ladies, even if the men were in their shirt sleeves."

"But they can't act!" asserted Mr. DeVere. "I have seen bills up advertising the moving pictures - all they seemed to be doing - the so-called actors, I mean - was falling off horses, roping steers - I believe "roping" is the proper term - or else jumping off bridges or standing in the way of railroad trains. And they call that acting!"

"Oh, you wouldn't have to do that, Daddy!" cried Alice, with a laugh. "Mr Pertell is putting on some real dramas - just like society plays, you know. Of course all the scenes won't take place in a parlor, I suppose. You won't have to do outdoor work, though, and I'm sure you won't have to catch a wild steer, or stop a runaway locomotive."

"I should hope not," he replied, with a tragic gesture.

"But that is real acting, all the same," went on Alice. In that little while she had come to have a great liking and interest in the moving picture side of acting. "You should see some of the scenes I saw. Why, Daddy, some of the men and women were just as good as some of the actors with whom you have been on the road."

"Oh, yes, if you include the road companies of the barn-storming days, perhaps," admitted Mr. DeVere. "But I refer to the real art of the drama, Alice. However, let us not discuss it. The subject is too painful. I have decided to take up the work, since I can do nothing else on account of my unfortunate voice - and I will do my best in the movies. It is due to myself that I should, and it is due to you girls that I provide for you in any way that I can."

"Oh, Dad!" exclaimed Ruth. "It is too bad if you have to sacrifice your art to mere bread and butter."

"Tut! Tut!" he exclaimed, smiling and holding up a chiding hand. "I don't look at it that way at all. I am not so foolish. Art may be a very nice thing, but bread and butter is better. We have to live, my dear. And, after all, my art is not so wonderful. I hope I have not exaggerated my worth to myself. I am very willing to try this new line, and I am very glad that Alice suggested it. Only it - it was rather a shock - at first. Now let us consider."

They talked it all over, and Alice went more into detail as to what she had seen at the moving picture theatre. Mr. DeVere grew more and more interested.

"It is very kind of Russ and Mr. Pertell to think of me," he said. "I will go and see this manager to-morrow."

The interview must have been a very satisfactory one, for Mr. DeVere returned from it with a smiling face - something he had not worn often since the failure of his voice.

"Well, Daddy?" queried Alice, as she entered the dining room, where she and Ruth were trying to make the most of a scanty supply of food. "How was it?"

For answer he pulled out a roll of bills - not a large one, but of a size to which the girls had not been accustomed of late.

"See, it is real money!" he cried, and he struck an attitude of one of the characters in which he had successfully starred. He was the old Hosmer DeVere once more.

"Where did you get it?" asked Ruth, with a little laugh. She foresaw that some of her housekeeping problems bade fair to be solved.

"It is an advance on my salary as a moving picture actor," he replied, hoarsely, but still with that same gay air. "See, I have put my other life behind me. Henceforth - or at least until my voice promises to behave," he went on, "I shall live, move and have my being on the screen. I have signed a contract with Mr. Pertell - a very fair contract, too, much more so than some I have signed with managers of legitimate theaters. This is part of my first week's salary. I have taken his money - there is no going back now. I have burned my bridges."

"And - are you sorry?" asked Alice, softly.

"No, little girl - no! I'm glad!" And truly he seemed so.

"Tell us about it," suggested Ruth, and he did - in detail.

"Then it wasn't so bad as you expected; was it, Daddy?" asked Alice.

"No, I found many of the company to be very fine characters, and some with exceptional ability. Mr. Wellington Bunn, by the way, is a man after my own heart."

"Oh, yes. He seemed very anxious to play Shakespeare," remarked Alice, with a smile. "I heard Mr. Pertell caution him about not letting Hamlet get into the parlor scene they were presenting," and she laughed at the recollection.

"Of course it was rather new and strange to me," went on Mr. DeVere, "but I dare say I shall get accustomed to it. There were some of the young ladies, though, for whom I felt no liking - Miss Pearl Pennington, who plays light leads, and her friend, Miss Laura Dixon, the ingenue."

"They were in vaudeville until recently," remarked Alice. "So Russ told me. Miss Pennington seemed very pretty."

"Passably so," agreed Mr. DeVere. "Well, our living problem is solved for us, anyway. Now I must study my new part. It is to be a sort of society drama, and will be put on in a few days. Mr. Pertell gave me some instructions. I shall have to unlearn many things that are traditional with those who have played all their parts in a real theatre. It is like teaching an old dog new tricks, but I dare say I shall master them."

"You're not really old, Daddy!" said Alice, slipping her arms about him, and nestling her cheek against his.

"There - there!" he returned, indulgently, "don't try to flatter your old father. You are just like your dear mother. Run along now, I must take up this new work. What a relief not to have to declaim my lines! I shall only move my lips, and who knows but, in time, my voice may come back?"

"I hope it will," answered Ruth, with a sigh. Somehow she could not quite bring herself to like her father in moving picture roles. Alice was entirely different.

"But, even if it does come back," said the younger girl, "you may like this new work so well, Dad, that you'll keep at it."

"Perhaps," he assented. "Here, Ruth, take care of this money – my first moving picture salary," and he handed her the bills.

As he went to his room with the typewritten sheets of his new part, Alice whispered to her sister:

"Hurray! Now we can have a real dinner. I'll go and buy out a delicatessen store."

The meal was a great success - not only from a gastronomic standpoint, but because of the jollity - real or assumed - of Mr. DeVere. He went over the lines of his new part, telling the girls how at certain places he was to "register," or denote, different emotions. "Register" is the word used in moving picture scenarios to indicate the showing of fear, hate, revenge or other emotion. All this must be done by facial expression or gestures, for of course no talking comes from the moving pictures - except in the latest kind, with a phonographic arrangement, and with that sort we are not dealing.

"Oh, I'm sure it will be fine!" cried Alice. "Can we go and see you act for the camera, Daddy?"

"Yes, I guess so," he replied. "Would you like it, Ruth?"

"I believe I should!" she exclaimed, with more interest than she had before shown. "It sounds interesting."

"Maybe we'll act ourselves, some day," added Alice.

"Oh, no!" protested her sister. "But let's sit down. The meal is spoiling. Oh!" she cried, with a hasty glance at the table. "Not a bit of salt. I forgot it. Alice, dear, just slip across the hall and borrow some from Mrs. Dalwood."

Humming, in the lightness of her heart, a little tune, Alice crossed to the apartment of their neighbor, not pausing after her first knock at the rear kitchen door.

She heard a rattling among the pots and pans, and naturally supposed Mrs. Dalwood was there.

"May we have some salt?" Alice called, as she entered the kitchen, but the next moment she drew back in surprise and fear, for a strange man, rising suddenly from under the sink, confronted her.

He, too, seemed startled.

"Oh - Oh!" gasped Alice. "Isn't Mrs. Dalwood here?"

"I - I believe not," stammered the man. "I - I'm the plumber - there's a leak -"

"Oh, excuse me," murmured Alice, but even in her embarrassment she could not help thinking that the man looked like anything but a plumber. She backed out of the kitchen, after picking up a salt cellar, and was more startled as she observed the man following her.

CHAPTER XI

RUSS IS WORRIED

Alice was racking her brain to recall where she had seen the man before. If he was a plumber, as he said he was, it might be that he had been in the apartment house on other occasions to repair breaks. But Alice was not certain.

"And yet I've seen him before, and lately, too," she thought. The girls was in the hall, now. The man, who seemed ill at ease, had followed and stood near.

"The leak wasn't a bad one; it is repaired now," he said.

"I - I didn't know Mrs. Dalwood was out," faltered Alice. And then, as the man turned to go down the stairs, like a flash it came to her who he was.

"The man Russ had the trouble with that day - Simp Wolley - who tried to get his patent!" Alice almost spoke the words aloud.

"The - the leak is fixed," the man went on.

"You - you -" stammered Alice. But the man did not stay to hear, but hurried downstairs.

Alice burst in on her sister and father.

"Oh!" she exclaimed. "That man - he - he was in the Dalwood kitchen!"

"What man?" asked Mr. DeVere, starting forward.

"The one who was after Russ's patent! Quick, can't you get him?"

Mr. DeVere ran into the hall, but the man had gone. The Dalwood kitchen door was still open, and a hasty look through the apartment showed none of the family could be at home.

"Could he have stolen the patent?" cried Alice, when the excitement had quieted down.

"We can't tell until Russ comes home," replied her father. "I'll leave our door ajar, and we can hear if anyone goes into the Dalwood rooms. As soon as some of them return we will tell them what has taken place."

Alice helped herself to the needed salt, and the meal began, with pauses now and then to learn if there was any movement in the flat across the hallway. Presently footsteps were heard, and proved to be those of Russ himself.

"Plumber!" he exclaimed. "So he was masquerading as that; eh?" the moving picture operator exclaimed when Alice told him what had occurred. "You're right, he was after my patent," and a worried look came over his face.

"Did he get it?" asked Ruth, anxiously.

"No, for it isn't here. The model is at a machine shop on the East Side, and several of the attachments are being made from it to be tested."

"Then it's all right," declared Alice, in a tone of relief.

"Yes - and no," returned Russ. "It's all right, for the time being, but I don't like what has happened. Simp Wolley must be getting desperate to come here in broad daylight and rummage the house under the pretense of being a plumber. It shows, too, that he must be watching this place, or he wouldn't have known when I went out."

"Hadn't you better notify the police?" suggested Mr. DeVere.

"I'll think about it," agreed Russ. "Of course he hasn't really done anything yet that they could arrest him for, unless coming into our apartment without being invited is illegal, and he could wriggle out of a charge of that sort. No, I'll keep my eyes open. In a little while, after I obtain my patent, and the attachment is on the market, he can't bother me. But I don't mind admitting that I'm worried."

"Then sit down and have something to eat with us," urged Alice, and Ruth, with a nod and a blush, seconded the request. "You'll be eating some of your own salt, anyhow," Alice suggested, in fun.

Russ lost a little of his apprehensive air as the meal progressed. Perhaps it was because Ruth sat opposite. Alice said as much to her sister afterward, when they were getting ready for bed.

"Don't be silly!" was Ruth's sole reply.

Mr. DeVere attended several rehearsals at the moving picture theater and, one morning, said:

"Girls, how would you like to come and see me in my new role? We have a dress rehearsal to-day, so to speak, and we'll "film" the play, as they call it, to-morrow."

"Oh, let's go, Ruth!" cried Alice, clapping her hands. "I know you'll enjoy it!"

"I'm sure I will," agreed Ruth. Her attitude toward the movies was also changing.

Together father and daughters went. It did Alice good to see how Mr. DeVere was welcomed by his fellow actors. He had already made himself friendly with most of them.

As Alice and Ruth came into the big studio, where a battery of cameras were clicking away, the two girls became aware of the looks cast at them by those not actually engaged in some scene. And, while most of the looks were friendly, those from two of the players were not.

Miss Pennington and Miss Dixon, standing together at one side of a section of a log cabin, whispered to each other.

"Ah, Mr. DeVere!" called Mr. Pertell. "Glad you're here; we were waiting for you."

"I hope I'm not late!" replied the actor, huskily, with a proper regard for not delaying a rehearsal.

"Oh, no. You're ahead of time if anything, and I'm glad of it. We'll have to set the smuggling play aside for a time. One of my men isn't here, and I can slip in your scenes now, and be that much ahead. So if you'll get ready we'll go on with 'A Turn of the Card.'"

"Yes, Mr. Pertell - certainly. Let me present you to my daughters. I believe you have met one."

"Yes - Miss Alice. I am glad to know the other one," and he bowed to Ruth. Then he hurried away. Mr. Pertell always seemed to be in a hurry.

Mr. DeVere went to his dressing room to don the costume of the character he was to represent - a wealthy banker - and Ruth and Alice gazed with interest at the various scenes going on about them.

While there were many persons connected with the Comet Film Company, there were certain principals who did most of the work. Among them, excepting Mr. DeVere, was Wellington Bunn, an old-time actor, who had long aspired to Hamlet, but who had given it up for the more certain income of the movies. Then there was Mrs. Margaret Maguire (on the bills as Cora Ashleigh) who did "old women" parts, and did them exceedingly well. She had two grandchildren, Tommy and Nellie, who were often cast for juvenile roles.

Carl Switzer was a joy to know. A German, with an accent that was "t'icker dan cheese," to use his own expression, he was a fund of happy philosophy under the most adverse circumstances. And on his round face was always a smile. He did the "comic relief," when it was needed, which was often.

Exactly opposite him in character was Pepper Sneed, the "grouch" of the company. Nothing ever went the way Pepper wanted it to go, from the depiction of a play to the meals he ate. No wonder he had dyspepsia. He was always apprehensive of something going to happen and when it did - well, they used to say that Pepper was the original "I told you so!"

Pearl Pennington and Laura Dixon have already been mentioned. Paul Ardite, who played opposite to Miss Dixon, was a good looking chap, with considerable ability. It was rumored that he and the ingenue - but there, I am not supposed to tell secrets.

Had it not been for "Pop" Snooks, I am sure the Comet Film Company would never have enjoyed the success it did. For Pop was the property man - the one of all work and little play. On him devolved the task of manufacturing at short notice anything from a castle to a police station.

And the best part of it was that Pop could do it. He was ingenuity itself, and they tell the story yet of how, when on the theatrical circuit, he made a queen's throne out of two cheese boxes and a board, and a little later in the same play, made from the same materials a very serviceable dog-cart.

As usual in the studio, several plays were going on at the same time - or, rather, parts of plays.

"Come on now!" called Mr. Pertell, sharply. "Get ready for that safe robbery scene. Pop, where's that safe?"

"It's being used as part of the wall in the dungeon in that 'Lord Scatterwait' scene," answered the property man.

"Well, hustle it over here, and get something else for the dungeon wall. I need that safe."

"That's the way it goes!" grumbled Pop as he scurried about. But that was all the fault he found, and presently the hole in the dungeon wall, caused by the removal of the safe with a painted canvas on it to represent stones, was filled by some boards taken from a fence used in a rural love drama.

"I say now, dot's not right!" spluttered Mr. Switzer, who as a country boy was making love to a country lass, (Miss Dixon). "Dot's not right, Pop. You dake our fence avay, und vat I goin' t' lean on ven I makes eyes at Miss Dixon? Ve got t' haf dot fence, yet!"

"I'll make you another in a minute!" cried Pop. "You don't go on for ten minutes."

"Mine gracious! Vot a business!" exclaimed the German, his round face showing as much woe as he ever allowed it to depict. "Dot vos a fine fence, mit der evening-glory vines trailing 'round mit it. Ach, yah!"

"Never mind," said Miss Dixon, "Pop will fix us up," and while she was waiting she strolled over to where Paul Ardite was talking to Alice. Russ Dalwood had come in and had greeted Ruth and Alice, and then, in response to an unseen gesture from Paul, had introduced him. Both girls liked the young fellow, who seemed quite interested in Alice.

"Are you going to play parts here?" asked Miss Dixon, with the freemasonry of the theater, speaking without being introduced.

"Oh, no!" replied Ruth, quickly. "We just came to see my father."

"Maybe they think they're too good for the movies," sneered Pearl Pennington, but only Russ heard her, and he glanced at her sharply.

"All ready for 'A Turn of the Card' now!" called Mr. Pertell, as Mr. DeVere came out of his dressing room. "Is your camera all ready, Russ?" for Russ had obtained a place with the film company, and had given up his position in the little moving picture theatre.

"All ready," was the answer. "I've got a thousand-foot reel in."

"Well, I don't want this particular scene to run more than eighty feet. Got to save most of the film for the bigger scenes. Now, watch yourselves, ladies and gentlemen. This is going to be one of our best yet, or I'm mistaken. Pop - where's Pop?"

"Here I am. What is it?"

"Get me a big armchair. I want Mr. DeVere to be sitting in that when the adventuress comes in. Miss Pennington, you're the adventuress, and I wish you'd look the part more."

"I'm doing the best I can."

"Well, fix your hair a little differently - a little more fluffy, you know - I don't know what you call it."

"Oh, that's easily remedied," she laughed. "I'm ready now," and with dexterous use of a side-comb she produced the desired result.

"Got that chair, Pop?" called the manager.

"Yep. Just as soon as I fix that fence for the rural scene."

"Yah! Py gracious, ve got t' haf our fence or dot love scene mit der evening-glory flowers vill be terrible!" insisted Mr. Switzer.

"All ready, now!" Mr. Pertell said, as the chair was placed in what was to represent a parlor. Mr. DeVere took his seat, and the action of the drama began. Ruth and Alice looked on with interest.

CHAPTER XII

THE PHOTO DRAMA

Mr. DeVere was an excellent actor. In his time he had played many parts, so the necessary action, or "business," as it is called, was not hard for him. He had learned readily what was expected of him, and though it seemed rather odd to make his gestures, his exits and entrances before nothing more than the eye of a camera, he soon had become accustomed to it after the days of rehearsal. And the great point was that he did not have to use his voice. Or, at the most, when some vital part of the little play called for speaking, he had only to whisper to give the "cue" to the others.

The plot was not a very complicated one, telling the story of a wealthy young fellow (played by Paul Ardite) the son of a wealthy banker, (Mr. DeVere) getting into bad company, and how he was saved by the influence of a good girl.

The "card" in question, was a visiting card, which seemed to compromise the young man, but the "turn" of it cleared him.

To save time, different scenes had already been set up in various parts of the big studio, and to these scenes - mere sections of rooms or offices - the actors moved.

With them moved Russ Dalwood, who was "filming" this particular play. He placed his little box-machine, on its tripod, before each scene, and used as many feet of film to get the succeeding pictures as Mr. Pertell thought was necessary.

I presume all my readers have seen moving pictures many times, and perhaps many of you know how they are made. But at the risk of repeating what is already known I will give just a little description of how the work is done.

In the first place there has to be a play to be "filmed," or taken. It may be a parlor drama an outdoor scene - anything from a burning building to a flood. With the play decided on, the actors and actresses for the different parts are selected and carefully rehearsed. This is necessary as the camera is instantaneous and one false move or gestures may spoil the film.

Next comes the selection of the location for the various scenes. Indoor ones are comparatively easy, for the scenic artist can build almost anything. But to get the proper outdoor setting is not so easy, and often moving picture companies go many miles to get just the proper scenery for a background.

So careful are some managers that they will send to California, or to the Holy Land, in order that their actors may have the proper historical surroundings. This costs many thousands of dollars, so it can be seen how important it is to get the film right at first.

There are two main parts to the moving picture business - the taking of the pictures and later the projection, or showing, of them on a white screen in some theatre.

For this two different machines are needed. The first is a camera, similar in the main principle to the same camera with which you may have taken snapshots. But there is a difference. Where you take one picture in a second, the moving picture camera takes sixteen. That is the uniform rate maintained, though there may be exceptions. And in your camera you take a picture on a short strip of celluloid film, or on a glass plate, but in the moving picture machine the pictures are taken on a narrow strip of celluloid film perhaps a thousand feet long.

The camera consists of a narrow box. On one side is a handle, and there is a lens that can be adjusted or focused. Inside is varied machinery, but I will not tire you with a description of it. Sufficient to say that there are two wheels, or reels. On one - the upper - is wound the unexposed film. One end of this film is fastened to the empty, or lower, reel. The film is passed back of lens, which is fitted with a shutter that opens and closes at the rate of sixteen times a second.

Turning a handle on the outside of the camera operates it. So that when the scene is ready to be photographed the actors, whether men or animals, begin to move. The handle turns, and the unexposed film is wound from one reel to the other, inside the camera, passing behind the lens, so that the picture falls on it in a flash, just as you take one snapshot. But, as I have said, the moving picture camera takes snapshot after snapshot - sixteen a second - until many thousands are taken, so that when the pictures are shown afterward they give the effect of continuous motion.

The film is moved forward by means of toothed sprocket wheels inside the camera, the shutter opening and closing automatically.

When the reel of film has all been exposed, it is taken to the dark room, and there developed, just as a small roll from your camera would be. This film is called the negative. From it any number of positives can be made, all depending on the popularity of the subject.

To make positives, the negative film is laid on another strip of sensitive celluloid of the same size. The two films are placed in a suitable machine, and then set in front of a bright light. The two films are then moved along so as to print each of the thousands of pictures previously taken.

The positive film is then developed, "fixed" to prevent it from fading, and it is then ready for the projecting machine. This latter is like the old-fashioned stereopticon, and by means of suitable lenses, and a brilliant light, the small pictures, hardly more than an inch square, are so magnified that they appear life-size on the screen.

That, in brief, is how moving pictures are made and shown, but it tells nothing of the hard work involved, on the part of operators, and actors and actresses. Often the performers risk their lives to make a "snappy" film, and many accidents have occurred where daring men and women took parts with wild beasts in the cast, or dared serious injury by long jumps.

Ruth and Alice watched their father enact his role. He did it well, and the girls were gratified to hear Mr. Pertell say from time to time:

"Good! That's the way to do it! Oh, that's great!"

The play was not a long one, but if it had taken three times the half-hour it consumed Ruth and Alice would not have been weary.

The last scene had been "filmed" by Russ, who was getting ready to take his camera to the dark room for development, when there came a crash from where Mr. Switzer was going through a love scene with Miss Dixon.

"Look out!" someone called.

There was a sound as of rending, splintering wood.

"Oh!" screamed Miss Dixon.

"Py gracious goodness!" ejaculated Mr. Switzer. "I am caught fast!"

"Oh, what has happened?" gasped Ruth, clinging to Alice.

"It sounded like an explosion!" the latter answered.

"Don't be alarmed," Russ assured them. "It's nothing. Only Switzer leaned too hard on that fence and it went down with him."

And that was what had happened. Amid the wreckage of the property fence, which had collapsed with the weight of the German actor, sat he and Miss Dixon, while the manager, with a gesture of despair exclaimed:

"That's another scene to be done over."

"I knew that would happen!" observed Pepper Sneed, gloomily.

CHAPTER XIII

MR. DEVERE'S SUCCESS

Amid laughter, now that it was seen that nothing serious had happened, the wreckage was cleared away, and the German actor, and his partner in the rural love scene, were assisted to their feet.

"Are you hurt?" asked Mr. Pertell, anxiously, when quiet had in a measure been restored.

"Only my feelings iss hurted!" replied Mr. Switzer, with an odd look on his round, fat face. "It iss not seemly und proper dot ven a feller is telling a nice girl vot he dinks of her, dot he should be upset head ofer heels alretty yet; ain't it?"

"It certainly is," agreed Miss Dixon, a little spasm of pain flitting across her face as she limped to one side.

"Oh, dear, I hope you're not hurt!" exclaimed Miss Pennington, hastening to her friend's side, and supporting her with an arm about her waist.

"It's only my ankle; it's a bit sprained, I think. A good thing I haven't a dancing part," said Miss Dixon.

"Will you be able to go on, when we make the film over again?" asked the manager anxiously. He did not make this inquiry because he was heartless, but the foremost thought with those who provide amusement for the public - whether they be managers or actors - is that "the show must go on." For that reason sickness, and even the death of loved ones, often does not stop the player from appearing on the stage. And, in a measure, this is no less so with those who help to make the moving pictures.

"Oh, I think I'll be able to go on after a bit," declared Miss Dixon, sinking into a chair that Pepper Sneed pushed forward for her.

"Go on! You'll never be able to go on inside of a week, little girl!" exclaimed the actor with the perpetual "grouch." He looked gloomily at those about him. "This is the worst business in the world," he went on. "Something is always happening. I know something will go wrong in that safe-blowing act I'm to do next. I -"

"Say, you go do that act, and then let us know if anything happens!" interrupted the manager. "They're waiting for you over there," and he motioned to an office setting, in which a safe robbery, one of the scenes of another play, was to take place.

"All right!" sighed Pepper Sneed, as he moved off to take his part. "But, mind what I'm telling you," he said to Miss Dixon. "You'll be laid up for a week."

"An' it all de fault of dot property man!" exclaimed Mr. Switzer. "He made dot fence like paper yet alretty! It vouldn't holt up a fly!"

"That was a good fence!" defended Pop Snooks. "The trouble was you leaned your ton weight on it."

"Ton veight! Huh! Vot you tink I am? A hipperperpotamusses? A ton veight - huh!" spluttered Mr. Switzer.

"Never mind now!" called the manager sharply, with a

reassuring glance at Ruth and Alice, who were regarding this little flurry with anxious eyes. They glanced over toward their father. "Pop, make a new fence - a strong one - and we'll film that scene over again," went on Mr. Pertell. "To your places, the rest of you. Mr. DeVere, I think that will be all we will require of you to-day. But come into the office. I have a new play I'm thinking of filming, and I'd like your advice on some of the scenes. Miss Dixon, shall I send for a doctor?"

"Oh, no, indeed, I'll be all right!" was her hasty answer.

"If you're not, don't be afraid to say so," spoke Mr. Pertell. "I can understudy you -"

"Oh, no, indeed!" she exclaimed, energetically. If there is one thing more than another that an actor or actress fears, it is being supplanted in a role. Of course, all the important parts in a play are "understudied"; that is, some other actor or actress than the principal has learned the lines and "business" so, in case the latter is taken ill, the play can go on, after a fashion. But players are jealous of one another to a marked degree, and rather than permit their understudy to succeed him, many a performer has gone on when physically unfit. Perhaps it was this that induced Miss Dixon to conceal the pain she was really suffering.

Mr. Pertell glanced sharply at her, and then his gaze roved to Ruth and Alice, who were standing with their father. A musing look was on the face of the manager. Miss Dixon saw it, and arose.

"I am perfectly able to go on, Mr. Pertell," she said, quickly. "There is no need of getting anyone in my place."

She walked across the room, with a slight limp, and the spasm of pain that showed on her face was quickly replaced by a smile. But it was an obvious effort.

Miss Dixon staggered, and would have fallen had not Alice

stepped forward quickly and caught her.

"You really ought to have a doctor," Alice said, anxiously. "A sprained ankle is sometimes quite serious."

"I don't need a doctor!" exclaimed the ingenue, sharply. "I shall be all right. It will take some little time to repair the fence, and by then -"

"You must let me attend to you," broke in a motherly voice, and Mrs. Maguire, who, as Cora Ashleigh, had finished her part in a little drama, came bustling over. "I'll put some hot compresses on your ankle, and that will take out the pain," went on the elderly actress. "Come along."

And Miss Dixon was glad enough to go. Mrs. Maguire was really a sort of "mother" to the others of the company, and many a physical ache and pain, as well as some mental ones, yielded to her ministering care.

"Now, then, Pop, how are you coming on with that fence?" asked the manager a little later.

"Oh, I'll get her done some time to-day if you don't give me too much else to do," was the answer. "But I've had to quit work on that trick auto you wanted - the one that turns into an airship."

"Pshaw! And I needed that, too. Well, go ahead. Do the best you can, and when you've finished I want a fake stone tower made for that fairy picture we're going to do next week."

"All right," agreed Pop. "I'll do it."

Nothing seemed too hard for him. He responded to the most exacting and diverse commands as easily as to the smallest. He was an invaluable property man.

"Oh, Mr. Ardite," continued the manager to the leading

juvenile, "I'm going to change your part in that runaway drama. I'll want some exterior scenes. One on the Brooklyn Bridge and another at the Grand Central Terminal. Get ready to go up there. Miss Fillmore will be here soon. She's in that with you. I'll send Charlie Blake up to film it. Here's the "register" list - look it over," and he tossed a sheaf of typewritten sheets to the young actor.

"I wish we could go see that taken," whispered Alice.

"You can, if you like," responded the manager, overhearing her.

"I - I'll be delighted to take you along," said Paul, coloring as he glanced at Alice.

Miss Dixon, who had come back from her room, after having her ankle bathed, looked up quickly at these words. She glanced from Alice to Paul, and back again, and then said something in a low voice to Miss Pennington.

"May I go, Daddy?" asked Alice. "I'm so interested in these moving pictures."

"Oh, yes, I think so," he assented. "Perhaps Ruth -"

"No, I'll go home with you," Ruth answered. "I'm a bit tired to-day."

"I'd never tire of this!" exclaimed Alice, with enthusiasm.

"Come along then!" invited Paul. "Here's Miss Fillmore now," he added, as another member of the company entered.

There was a sudden cry of pain from the other side of the studio, and a moving picture camera ceased clicking.

"What's the matter now?" asked the manager, as he looked to where the safe robbery scene was being filmed.

"Oh, I caught my hand in the safe door!" exclaimed Pepper Sneed. "Nearly took my finger off! I just knew something would happen to me to-day!"

"Great Scott! Another scene spoiled!" groaned Mr. Pertell. "Well, do it over. Had you run out much film?" he asked the operator.

"No, only a few feet."

"Well, try again. And, Pepper, look out for your head this time, that you don't get that caught in the safe. You might lose it."

"Uh!" grunted the human grouch.

Russ Dalwood came out of the developing room.

"That's going to be a great film!" he declared. It's one of the best I've ever seen. The pictures will show up fine."

"Glad to hear it," remarked the manager. "That's some good news in this day of trouble."

"Did I do all right?" asked Mr. DeVere, hoarsely. "I would like to see myself - as others see me - and that's possible now, in the movies."

"Your pictures are fine," answered Ross.

"And I want to congratulate you," went on Mr. Pertell. "You are doing splendid work, and we are glad to have you with us. It is not everyone who can come from the legitimate stage and go into the movies with success; but you have."

"I am glad to hear it," declared the actor. "There was great necessity, or I should not have done it; but I am not sorry now. It is a great relief not to have to speak my lines."

"And you mustn't do much talking now, Daddy," cautioned Ruth. "You want your throat to get well, you know."

"Yes, I know, dear," replied her father, patting her on the shoulder.

"Good-bye!" called Alice, who with Paul, Miss Fillmore, and the camera operator, were going out for the exterior scenes. "I'll be home soon."

"I'll take care of her," promised Paul, and, as he and Alice went out, side by side, Ruth caught a sharp glance from Miss Dixon, who was narrowly watching the two.

"Well, everything seems to be going on all right now," observed Mr. Pertell. "Here's Pop with the fence. Now, Mr. Switzer, and Miss Dixon - well, what is it?" he broke off with, as he saw Wellington Bunn approaching with an irritated air.

"I must refuse, sir, positively refuse, to go on with the part you have assigned to me!" exclaimed the former Shakespearean player, striking what he thought was a dignified attitude. "I cannot do it, Mr. Pertell, and I wonder that you expect it of me."

"What part is it you object to?" asked the manager. "Let's see, you're in 'A Man's Home;' aren't you?"

"Yes, and in one scene I am supposed to come home from the office, and get down on the floor to play with blocks with the children. I do not mind that so much, but I have to play horse, and ride the children around on my back, and then, to cap the climax, I have to turn a somersault."

"Well?" asked the manager, as the actor paused.

"Well, I positively refuse to do that somersault! The idea of me - Wellington Bunn - who has played in Shakespearean dramas, groveling on the floor and turning somersaults! The somersaults positively must be cut out."

"But they can't very well, Mr. Pertell!" broke in one of the other actors in the same drama. "Because when Mr. Bunn goes over that way he is supposed accidentally to upset the table, and the supper things fly all over, and the children laugh and think it's a great joke. The whole scene will be spoiled if Mr. Bunn doesn't turn his somersault."

"Then he'll turn it!" announced the manager, grimly.

"What! But I protest, sir! I protest!" cried the tragedian. "I will not do it! The idea of me - Wellington Bunn -"

"Somersault - or look for another engagement," was the terse rejoinder, and with a gesture of despair Mr. Bunn turned aside murmuring;

"Oh, that I should come to this! Oh, the pity of it! The pity! I'll never do it!"

But a little later, for the sake of his salary, he turned the somersault.

CHAPTER XIV

AN EMERGENCY

"Did you enjoy yourself, Alice?" asked Ruth, a little later that afternoon, when her sister had returned from her trip to the Brooklyn Bridge, and the Grand Central Terminal, with Paul.

"Indeed I did!" replied the younger girl. "It was really exciting. And Paul is so nice!"

"Do you call him Paul?"

"Certainly - why not."

"And does he call you Alice?"

"Yes. He asked me if he couldn't, and I don't see any harm. He's just like a brother would be."

"Oh," remarked Ruth, with a little smile. "Tell me about it."

"Oh, there isn't much to tell. We went up in a car until we got to where the scenes were to be filmed. Then Paul and Miss Fillmore did what they had to do, and the pictures were taken.

"There was quite a crowd looking, on, too, and some of them got in the pictures," Alice went on.

"Purposely, do you mean - to spoil them?" asked Ruth.

"Oh, no, they belonged in. You see this was supposed to be a natural scene of Paul and Miss Fillmore meeting on the bridge. They walk along a little way, and part of the plot develops there. So there had to be other persons walking along to make it look natural. How odd it must be if those same persons happen to see the film play later, and recognize themselves in the pictures."

"Rather, I should say," agreed Ruth. "What next?"

"Oh, then we went up to the Grand Central, and there Paul had to pretend to get on a train, and Miss Fillmore bade him a tearful good-bye. She's quite an emotional actress, too.

"It was quite exciting. Paul had some work getting the station master to let us out on the train platform without tickets. But when he explained about the moving pictures, it was all right.

"It was as real as anything - just as if it wasn't for the films at all. Paul got on the platform, and a porter took someone else's grip to make it look as though he were going on a journey.

"That porter enjoyed it more than anyone else. He grinned so much that Paul had to tell him to stop, or the top of his head might come off. And laugh! I wish you could have heard him laugh at that. It took us a little longer to get those films, for there was such a crowd. But it was all right. I've had a lovely time!" cried Alice, her brown eyes brilliant with excitement, and her cheeks flushed.

"And what happened next?" asked Ruth, after a pause.

"Oh, Miss Fillmore had an engagement, so Paul and I went and had lunch together. He's an awfully nice boy!"

"Alice!"

"I don't care; he is! And he's in papa's company, so I don't see any harm - especially as it was in daylight, and it was only in one of those dairy lunches, you know. Paul wanted to take me to a better place, but I know he doesn't earn much yet, and I wasn't going to have him waste his money."

"Thoughtful of you," murmured Ruth.

"Wasn't it. Where's daddy?"

"Oh, he went back to the studio. There was some mistake in one of his acts and he wanted to have it corrected so he could study over it to-night."

"Oh, hasn't it been a day!" exclaimed Alice, as she laid aside her hat. "Do you know, I think outdoor pictures are better, and more interesting. I'd like to be in some myself."

"It is interesting," agreed Ruth. "And really it doesn't seem like acting when you don't have any audience except a camera. But I suppose that makes it all the more difficult. Russ was in a little while ago."

"What did he want?" asked Alice with a quick glance at her sister.

"Oh, he just called to say that all the films in which dad appears came out fine. He mentioned that his patent was coming on all right, and he expects soon to have it out on royalty."

"That's nice. I do hope those horrid men won't get it away from him. What have we to eat? I'm nearly starved."

"Why, I thought you had lunch."

"I did, but we - we took a walk afterward, and my appetite came back."

Ruth looked curiously at Alice, sighed and then went out to the kitchen.

As the days went on Mr. DeVere grew to like his new occupation more and more. At first he had talked and mused over the coming time when he could go back to the regular theatre. But his voice showed no tendency to lose its whispering hoarseness, and he was, perforce, compelled to do his acting for the camera. Then came a gradual change of feeling, and he grew really to like his new occupation. Besides, it paid almost as well as a legitimate role, and was more certain.

The girls and their father enjoyed a private view of the film in which Mr. DeVere was depicted. It was an absorbing play, and while it seemed a bit uncanny, at first, to look at yourself moving about, Mr. DeVere grew accustomed to it.

"And it is surprising what faults one can see in onesself," he remarked, after the film had been thrown on the screen for him. "I can pick out a number of places where I can improve in my gestures. And I see places where the action can be more easily and plainly explained to the audience."

"I am glad you do," spoke Mr. Pertell. "It is a good thing to try to improve the movies. They have, in my opinion, a great lesson to teach to the masses, as well as to provide amusement for them. And all we can do, individually, to help, adds to it.

"I am thinking of greatly broadening my fields, I am not satisfied to film merely parlor dramas and a few city scenes. I want a larger scenic background, and I'm working to that end."

"I hope I shall be able to fit into some of them," observed Mr. DeVere. "I, too, begin to think I would like to get out in the open."

"I intend to have you with me," declared the manager. "I am looking around for a locality to serve as a background for certain rural plays. But I have not found it yet."

Ruth and Alice paid many visits to the film studio, and

watched the making of many plays. Their father had parts in a number of them, and for others new actors were engaged temporarily.

Russ was becoming an expert operator, and meanwhile was working on his patent. It was nearly perfected.

They were exacting days that followed. Many dramas had to be filmed, and all the actors and actresses were kept busy. Ruth and Alice spent many afternoons in the studio, growing more and more interested all the while. There was much fun, as well as much hard work, for Mr. Switzer, with his odd expressions and mishaps, was a source of considerable amusement.

Then, too, the "human grouch," Pepper Sneed, seemed always to find some new objection to raise, or some dire calamity to predict. And as for Mr. Bunn, he made many protests at roles he considered incongruous with his dignity.

Once he wanted the story of a play so changed that he might give an impersonation of Hamlet in a setting that included a Western mining cabin, and when he was refused by the manager he grew quite indignant.

"You might as well try to introduce Macbeth in the clown act," declared Mr. Pertell.

Several times Ruth and Alice had expressed a desire to try a little part in one of the dramas, but their father would not listen. At last, however, their chance came.

Mr. DeVere had just completed his role in a difficult part, and Russ, with his camera, had been shifted over to film another play, a few of the scenes of which were laid in the studio, the others being set out of doors.

"Well, aren't those two young ladies here yet?" asked Mr. Pertell, coming out of his office, as he noted a delay.

"Not yet," answered Mrs. Maguire, who was to have a part in the act. "They said they'd be early, too."

"That's always the way when you want someone in a hurry," stormed the manager. "Here we are holding things up just because Miss Parker and Miss Dengon aren't here. It wouldn't taken them five minutes to do their parts, either."

"Well, I can't wait much longer," said the principal actor, who was to take a part with the young ladies who were missing. "I've got to get that train, you know, Pertell."

"Yes, I know!" was the answer, as the manager snapped shut his watch. "I can't see what's keeping them. This gets on my nerves!"

"What is it?" asked Mr. DeVere, coming from his dressing room. "Anything I can do to help you?"

"No, but two extra young girls I hired for certain parts are missing, and this thing ought to go on. Harrison has an important engagement, and can't wait either. I didn't count on this emergency, though usually I allow for delays. If I only had two girls now - Say!" he cried, as he looked over at Ruth and Alice. "They might do it - they might fill in! How about it, Mr. DeVere; would you let them substitute in this drama? It's a simple thing, and with two minutes' coaching they can do it. That will let Harrison get his train, and I can go on with the next scenes. Will you girls try?" he asked, appealing to them.

CHAPTER XV

JEALOUSIES

Alice hesitated, but only a moment, and, while Ruth was looking at her father, the younger girl exclaimed:

"Oh, do let us try! I don't know that we could do it, Mr. Pertell, but let us try! Won't you, Daddy?"

Mr. DeVere looked troubled. For some time past he had been watching the growing liking of his daughters for the moving pictures, and he was in two minds about the matter. He had seen that this new manner of presenting plays had a great future, not only for the public but for the acting profession. And now, when a chance came for his daughters to get into it, he hardly knew what to say. He had made up his mind that they should never go on the dramatic stage. But this - .

"Something has to be done," urged the manager. "I can't hold things back much longer."

"Wouldn't you like to try it, Ruth?" asked Alice, catching her sister's hands. "I think it will be just fine!"

"Why, I - I think I would like it - if they think I can do it," agreed Ruth.

"Oh, you can do it all right," Mr. Pertell assured her. "It is very simple. A little coaching is all you need. What do you say,

Mr. DeVere? May the girls go in?"

"Why, I - er - I hardly know what to say. It is so different from anything they have ever done. And I never expected -"

"Oh, they can do it!" interrupted the manager. "They've been around here long enough to know how we do things. Come, it may be a good opening for them."

"All right, I don't mind," said the actor. "I shall be very glad to let them help you out, Mr. Pertell."

"Oh, I don't ask it as a favor. I'm willing to pay for their time. I was to give Miss Parker and Miss Dengon five dollars each for a few minutes of their time to-day, but they have disappointed me. I now offer it to your daughters."

"Oh, fine!" cried Alice, clapping her hands. "Then I can get that new hat I've been wanting so much. Come on, Ruth. What do we have to do, Mr. Pertell?"

The manager quickly explained what was wanted. The two girls had simple parts, with Mr. Harrison as the chief character. Alice and Ruth soon grasped what was required of them, and, after a little coaching and rehearsing, they were ready.

"Now stand over here," directed Mr. Pertell, who took personal charge this time, "and don't pay any attention to the camera. Don't look at it, in fact. Keep your eyes on Mr. Harrison, or on some part of scenery. Just forget everything but what you have to do."

"Shall we speak the lines aloud?" asked Ruth.

"If you like. Perhaps it will be better, for the first time, to do so," suggested Mr. Pertell. "It may help you to get the 'business' down better. A little more light here!" he called to the electrician, for in one of the scenes artificial illumination was used. "Are you all ready, Russ?" he asked the young operator.

"All ready; yes, sir!"

"Then - go!"

The little section, from what was to be a two-reel play of the movies, was under way. Though a bit nervous Ruth and Alice did very well, and soon they were in the swing of it.

When it came time for Alice to act the part of a hoydenish character, she was exceedingly natural in it, and her laugh at the simulated discomfiture of Mr. Harrison was so spontaneous that even some of the others joined in.

Ruth, too, who had a more demure part, acquitted herself well. The camera clicked on, Russ turning the handle steadily. He nodded reassuringly at Ruth when she had a moment's respite.

Then came a slight change of scene, and a change of costume on the part of the girls, Mrs. Maguire finding just what was needed in the wardrobe of the studio.

Then, just as the final strip of film had been exposed, and the emergency work of Ruth and Alice had ended, in came the two tardy actresses.

"You're too late!" exclaimed Mr. Pertell. "We couldn't wait for you."

"What!" exclaimed Miss Parker. "Do you mean to tell us you went and filmed our parts with somebody else in the cast?"

"That's what we did," replied the manager, coolly. "Maybe you'll learn after this that four o'clock means four o'clock, and not half past."

"Well, what do you know about that?" gasped Miss Dengon, sinking into a plush chair, and dabbing at her nose with a chamois skin, which gave off puffs of powder like a miniature gun.

"An' us tryin' as hard as ever we could to get here!" went on Miss Parker, vigorously chewing gum. "The nerve of some people is suttinly amazin'! Come on, Ruby, I never did care much for movies anyhow, an' how some folks can stay in 'em is suttinly a mystery to me!"

Then, with heads held high, and with meaning glances at Miss Pennington and Miss Dixon, who were busy in another drama, the two young ladies went out, looking superciliously at Ruth and Alice.

"Business is business - in the movies the same as anywhere else," chuckled Mr. Pertell, as he gave Ruth and Alice each a crisp five-dollar bill. "I am very much obliged to you, in the bargain," he went on.

"So am I!" added Mr. Harrison. "I can get my train now, and it's a satisfaction to know that the scenes are completed."

"Oh, it was fun!" laughed Alice.

"I liked it, too," confessed Ruth.

"And I want to tell you that you both did most excellently," said the manager. "You have a very good grasp of what is wanted, and you put in the 'business' very naturally. I congratulate you and your father," and he nodded to Mr. DeVere.

"I have given them a little instruction in the fundamentals," confessed the actor, "and of course they have been about the theatre, more or less, since they were small children."

"I suppose that accounts for it," observed Mr. Pertell. "Well, I want to say that I am very much pleased with you, and, if you think you would like to try it again, I can make parts for you in a drama that I am going to film next week."

"Oh, Ruth! Let's do it!" begged Alice.

Ruth looked at her father inquiringly.

"What sort of parts are they?" he asked.

"Oh, very much the same as they undertook to-day, only longer and more elaborate. There will be several changes of scene and costume. Do you think you'd like it?"

"Like it? I'd love it!" cried Alice, gaily, "Do say we may, Daddy dear!" and she put her arms around his neck.

"I'll see," was all he would promise. "I must look over the parts, and then - well, little coaching wouldn't do you any harm, I guess," he added with a smile.

"It would make them all the better," declared the manager.

"Oh, Ruth! I believe he's going to let us go in!" whispered Alice in delight. "Won't you like it?"

"Yes, dear! It's more exciting than I imagined. And I think you did splendidly!"

"Not half as well as you, Ruth. You are a born actress!"

"And you're a born ingenue!"

"Oh, aren't we silly to compliment each other this way!" laughed Alice. "But, really, Ruth, I just love it; don't you?"

"Yes, dear. Oh, I wonder what sort of parts we'll get. I'd like something romantic."

"And I want something funny - with laughs in it," declared Alice. "Oh, say, Ruth," and her voice went to a whisper, "do you really think I'm an ingenue - like Miss Dixon?"

"I think you're - better!" responded Ruth, kissing her sister, and stroking her soft hair.

The work in the film studio was over for the day and the actors and actresses were getting ready to go home. From the time Ruth and Alice had taken the emergency parts Russ had observed Miss Pennington and Miss Dixon casting sharp looks at them.

"Jealous!" mused Russ. And his diagnosis was confirmed a little later, when, as the two former vaudeville performers passed Ruth and Alice, Miss Pennington, with a sharp glance at the latter, murmured loudly enough to be heard:

"Humph! It takes more than one performance in a little part to make a movie actress! Some folks think they are mighty smart, coming in over the heads of others!"

"That's what I say, too!" added Miss Dixon. "It was a shame the way they took the parts away from Ruby and Maude!"

CHAPTER XVI

THE MOVING PICTURE GIRLS

For a moment Ruth and Alice looked at each other with eyes that showed the pain they felt. Ruth turned pale at hearing the unkind words, but Alice blushed a rosy red, and started to say something.

"Don't," advised Mrs. Maguire, coming up beside them, and evidently guessing her intention. "It would only make matters worse to reply to them, my dear."

"But - but -" began Alice.

"Hush!" begged Ruth. "Oh, how could they say it - as if we *wanted* to displace those girls."

"I'm just going to tell them what I think!" exclaimed Alice, and there was a hint of real anger in her voice. But she had no chance, for Miss Pennington and Miss Dixon, as though satisfied with what they had done, swept out to the elevator.

"Don't mind them, my dears," said motherly Mrs. Maguire. "It's only professional jealousy, anyhow; and you'll see plenty of that if you stay in this business long enough."

"Then I'm not going to stay!" cried Alice. "I'm not used to having such things said of me."

Mrs. Maguire laughed genially. She was standing with Ruth and Alice, who were waiting for their father to join them. Most of the other performers had now gone.

"Oh, you'll get so you won't mind that a bit!" went on Mrs. Maguire. "Sure, I used to eat my heart over it in my younger days, but now I only laugh. It's part of the business. It's a tribute to your acting, my dear, and you ought to take it as such. Don't mind it."

"Oh, but it was so - so uncalled - for!" murmured Ruth. "I think I must -"

"Hush! Here comes daddy!" interrupted Alice. "Don't let him know about it."

"That's wise," commented Mrs. Maguire. "Though probably he's seen enough of it in his time. But perhaps he wouldn't like to know that it bothered you. Best say nothing to him, my dears. It will wear away soon enough."

"No, we won't say anything," agreed Alice, slipping her arm through her sister's. "Papa has enough trouble as it is."

A little later, as the girls were walking along with Mr. DeVere, he asked them:

"Well, how did you like your parts in the movies?"

"Fine. It was so interesting, Dad!" exclaimed Ruth.

"I'd like to do some more!" echoed Alice, with a meaning look at her sister.

"Well, I must see what sort of parts Mr. Pertell will cast you for," said Mr. DeVere. "But I am glad you like the work. It may be a great deal better for all of us to be in this than if I was alone in a regular theater. We can always be together now, and certainly my voice doesn't seem to be improving very fast."

This was only too true. Several visits to the physician, and a heroic course of treatment, had resulted in only a slight improvement. The pain in the vocal chords had been lessened, but the huskiness remained, so that it would have been practically impossible for Mr. DeVere to speak his lines in a regular theater. So the moving pictures were suited to him.

The DeVere family was now in much better circumstances than when we first made their acquaintance. They had been gradually paying the back bills, the landlord had been appeased, so that there was no danger of dispossession, and there was much happiness in the little flat.

"We could even afford a better one, if you girls would like to move," said Mr. DeVere one day.

"Oh, no, let's stay," suggested Ruth. "We can save a little money by remaining here, and paying less rent."

"Besides, we have such nice neighbors!" observed Alice, with a glance at the Dalwood apartments across the hall, at the same time giving Ruth a sly nudge.

"Stop it!" commanded Ruth. "What do you mean, Alice?"

"Just what I said - we have *such* nice neighbors across the way," and she gave a little pinch to her sister's blushing cheek.

"Yes, the Dalwoods are very good friends," remarked Mr. DeVere, all unconscious of this little by-play between his daughters. "And Russ is certainly a fine young man."

"Indeed he is; isn't he, Ruth?" asked Alice tantalizingly.

"Oh, yes, I suppose so," was the blushing answer. "But how should I know - any more than you do about Paul Ardite?" and she glanced shrewdly at Alice.

"A hit, I suppose you would call that. A Roland for my Oliver, my dear!" laughed Alice, frankly. "I don't mind."

She looked toward her father, but he was so absorbed in looking over a new part he was to take, that he paid little attention to the chatter of the girls.

A few days after the first appearance of Ruth and Alice before the moving picture camera, in the small roles they had taken to bridge over an emergency, Mr. Pertell brought them their parts in a new drama. Meanwhile it had been ascertained that the films where the girls filled in had been a success. Ruth and Alice felt a little diffident about going to the studio again, especially after the scene with the jealous actresses.

But Miss Dixon and Miss Pennington appeared to have gotten over their pique, and they acted as though they had never said anything to wound or annoy Ruth and Alice. The latter, however, could not forget it, and were rather cool toward their fellow-players.

"Here are your new parts," said Mr. Pertell. "Look them over with your father as soon as you can. He is to be in the play with you."

"Oh, isn't this exciting!" cried Alice, as she took the typewritten manuscript. "Real parts at last, Ruth!"

"Yes. We will be real actresses if we keep on. I wonder what I am cast for?"

"My! We're becoming quite adept in theatrical talk. Ahem!" laughed Alice with pretended sarcasm.

Miss Pennington and Miss Dixon, who were already rehearsing for another play, looked over at the two enthusiastic sisters, and shrugged their shoulders.

"Wait until they have been in it as long as we have, my dear, then they won't be so jolly," remarked Miss Pennington.

"Oh, I don't know as you can include me," was Miss Dixon's rather tart comment. "*I* haven't been at it so many years."

"Oh, haven't you?" asked Miss Pennington, with a raising of her penciled eyebrows. "Excuse me, my dear!"

"Don't mention it!"

"Get on to that, would you!" exclaimed Pop Snooks to Mr. Sneed. "The two old-timers are scrappin'."

"I knew they would," was the grouchy rejoinder. "They'll have a real quarrel, and both quit, and that'll mean some new members in the company. And just as we are about through rehearsing that piece, and about to film it, too. That means I'll have to do it all over again. I knew something would happen!"

"Oh, cheer up! The worst is yet to come!" laughed Paul Ardite. "Here's Switzer looking as red as a lobster. What is it now, Carl?" he asked.

"Ach! Vot isn't der matter?" cried the moon-faced one. "I haf a part vot incessitates me to be bound und gagged by a band of robbers, und stood in a corner vhile dey loot der blace."

"Well, that's a nice, romantic part," observed Paul.

"Yah, but how would you like to haf a rag stuffed in your mout so vot you couldn't breath yet for five minutes? How vould you like dot; hey? Dell me dot!"

"Oh, well, tell 'em to leave you a breathing hole," laughed Paul.

"Where is Mr. Pertell? Where is he? I demand to see him at once!" broke in the voice of Wellington Bunn. "I must see him instantly!"

"He was here a moment ago, giving the Misses DeVere their

parts," replied Paul. "Why, is the place on fire?"

"No, but I refuse to take the part he has assigned to me. I utterly and positively refuse to so demean myself."

"What part have you?" asked the young fellow, looking over at Alice and nodding.

"Why, he has cast me - I, who have played all the principal Shakespearean characters - he has cast me - Wellington Bunn - as a waiter in a hotel scene! Where is Mr. Pertell? I refuse to take that character!"

"Oh, what's the trouble now?" asked the manager, coming from his office. The Shakespearean actor explained.

"Now see here!" exclaimed Mr. Pertell, with more anger than he usually displayed. "You'll take that part, Mr. Bunn, or leave the company! It is an important part, and has to do with the development of the plot. Why, as that waiter you intercept the taking of ten thousand dollars, and prevent the heroine from being abducted. Afterward you become rich, and blossom out as a theatrical manager."

"And do I produce Shakespeare?" asked the old actor, eagerly.

"There's nothing to stop you - in the play," returned Mr. Pertell, rather drily.

"Oh, then it's all right," said Mr. Bunn, with a sigh of relief. "I'll take the part."

Rehearsals were going on in various parts of the studio, and some plays were being filmed. Russ Dalwood was busy at one of the cameras.

"Have you got a part you like, Ruth?" asked Alice, when she had finished looking over her lines.

"Indeed I have, I'm supposed to be Lady Montgomery, and there are two counts in love with me. At least, one is a count and the other pretends to be one. It's quite romantic. What is yours?"

"Mine's jolly. I'm a school girl, always up to some trick or other, and - yes, see here - why in one of my tricks I disclose that the pretended count who's in love with you is only an organ grinder! Oh, that will be fun," and she laughed gleefully.

"Do you like your parts?" asked the manager, coming up.

"Indeed we do!" chorused Ruth and Alice.

"Then talk to your father about them," he advised. "See what he says, and if he is willing you may begin rehearsals with him, and the others of the cast."

Mr. DeVere was fully satisfied with the parts assigned to his daughters, and agreed to allow them to enter formally into the work of the moving pictures at a very fair salary for beginners. The others of the company were called together, including Paul Ardite, and the best method of getting the finest results out of the drama was discussed.

In the days that followed, Ruth and Alice, as well as the others, did hard work. It is not as easy to go through a moving picture play as it appears merely from seeing the film on the white curtain. Some scenes have to be rehearsed over and over again, and often, after being filmed, some defect results and the work has to be all done once more.

Mr. DeVere rehearsed his daughters at home in the intervals of their appearance at the studio, and this redounded to their benefit. They were thus able to do effective work, and Mr. Pertell complimented them on it.

The play was soon ready for filming, and Russ was chosen to work the camera. Some of the scenes were out of doors, in a big flower garden, and for this the company was taken to Brooklyn, where a private owner was induced to allow his place to be used for a few minutes. Ruth and Alice enjoyed their part in the flower garden very much.

Finally the last rehearsal was had, and the day was set for making the films of the first real, big play in which the two girls had ever taken part. As they were leaving the studio together, on the afternoon of the day before the first "performance," they saw a group of children standing down near the main entrance.

"There go some of the moving picture girls now," one boy exclaimed.

"Don't I wish I was them!" sighed a tall, lanky girl next him. "Ain't they nice, Jimmie?"

"They sure is!" was the enthusiastic rejoinder.

"We're achieving fame, Ruth," laughed Alice.

"Such as it is - yes," replied her sister. "'Moving picture girls'; eh? Well, I suppose we are."

CHAPTER XVII

A PROMISE

"Now then, are we all ready?" asked Mr. Pertell. He looked about the studio, at the groups of actors and actresses, at the camera men - particularly at Russ. "Everybody here?" he went on.

"All here," replied Pop Snooks, checking off a list he held.

"How about your props?"

"Nothing missing, not even the firecracker Miss Alice sets off under the chair of the false count," replied the property man.

"Good! I don't want any failure at the last minute. Now, Russ, how is the camera working?"

"Fine, sir."

"Good fresh film?"

"Fresh to-day, Mr. Pertell - just like new-laid eggs."

"All right. You may have a chance to snap some newly laid eggs if my future plans work out all right. Well, I guess we'll begin. Take your places for the first scene."

"Oh, I'm so nervous!" confided Ruth to Alice.

"Silly! You needn't be!" was the response. "You're just perfect in your part. I only wish I was as sure of myself."

"Why, you're great, Alice!" said her sister. "Only you do such funny things - it makes me laugh, and I'm afraid I'll smile in the wrong place - when I'm being made love to, for instance."

"Well, it's a funny part, and I have to act funny," insisted the younger girl. "But I wish it was all over, and on the films. It's been a little harder than I thought it would be."

"Indeed it has. But papa was so good to rehearse us. Now we must be a credit to him."

"Oh, of course. Come on, the others are ready."

It was not without a feeling of nervousness that Ruth and Alice prepared to take their places in the actual depiction of the new play. The rehearsals had not been so trying; but now, when the photographs were to be made, there was a strain on all.

For in making moving pictures mistakes are worse than on the real stage. There, when one is speaking, one can correct a false line, or turn it so that the audience does not notice the "break."

But in the movies a false move, a wrong gesture, is at once indelibly registered on the film, to reappear greatly magnified. And though sometimes the incorrect part of the film can be cut out, mistakes are generally costly.

"Are you all ready?" asked Mr. Pertell again, as he stood with watch in hand beside Russ at the camera, while the actors and actresses took their places in the first scene.

"All ready," answered Mr. Harrison, who was one of the principal characters.

"Then - go!" cried the manager, and Russ was about to turn

the operating handle.

"Vait! Vait a minute. Holt on!" cried the voice of Mr. Switzer. "Don't shoot yet alretty!" and he held up a restraining hand.

"Oh, what's the matter now?" demanded Mr. Pertell, with a gesture of annoyance.

"Vun of mine shoes - he iss unloose, und der lacing is dingle-dangling. It might trip me!" explained the good-natured German actor, in all seriousness.

"Well, fix it, and hurry up!" cried the manager, unable to repress a smile.

"Yah! I tie her goot und strong," he said, and soon this was done.

"Now then - all ready?" asked Mr. Pertell once more.

This time there was no delay, and the clicking of the camera was heard as Russ turned the handle. Mr. DeVere and his two daughters were not in this first scene, so it gave the girls a chance to lose some of their nervousness - or "stage fright." As for Mr. DeVere, he was too much of a veteran actor to mind this. Besides, he had played many parts before the camera now.

Mr. Pertell stood with watch in hand, timing the performance. For the play must be gotten on a certain length of film, and if one scene ran over its allotted time it might spoil the next one by curtailing the action.

"Hurry a little with that," ordered the manager sharply, at a certain point. "Don't 'screen' the letter too long, and skip part of that leave-taking. That eats up far too much celluloid."

Accordingly some parts, not essential to the play, were "cut" to shorten the time. Russ went on turning the crank, getting hundreds of the tiny pictures that afterward would be magnified, and thrown on the screen in dozens of moving picture playhouses, for the Comet Company supplied a large "circuit."

"Now then, Mr. DeVere, it's time for you to come on," the manager said. "And then your daughters."

"Oh, I know I'm going to be nervous!" murmured Ruth.

"No you won't," spoke Russ, encouragingly. She stood near him, and flashed him a grateful look. "I'll be watching you," he said, "and if I see anything wrong I'll stop in an instant, so we won't spoil any film."

"That's good of you," she replied. "Come on, Alice."

"All right! Oh, I just know it's going to be splendid!" her sister exclaimed. There was the flush of excitement on her cheeks, and though she would not admit, Alice, too, was nervous. So much, she felt, depended on this first real play - so much for herself and her sister. It was thrilling to feel that they might be able to make a comfortable living through the medium of the movies.

"All ready now, Russ, for this scene," called the manager, indicating the one where Ruth and Alice were to appear. "Watch your register closely."

"Yes, sir."

The play went on. Ruth took her part first, and the little drama was enacted. Her father, who was in the scene with her, smiled encouragement, and Russ nodded gaily as he continued to turn the clicking camera.

"Now, Miss Alice!" called the manager. "Here's where you come in. Come smiling!"

It was hardly necessary to tell Alice this, for she generally had a smile on her face. Nor was it lacking this time.

She began her part, but in an instant the manager called:

"Wait. Hold on a minute!"

The clicking of the camera ceased instantly.

"Oh, have I done something wrong?" thought Alice, her heart beating violently.

"Cut out what's been done so far," ordered the manager to Russ. "It will have to be done over."

"Yes, sir," answered the operator, as he noted from the automatic register at the side of the camera how many feet of film had been run on the new scene. Then, when it came to be developed, it could be eliminated. The figures also showed how much of the thousand-foot reel was left for succeeding scenes.

Everyone was a little nervous, fearing he or she had made the trouble, but all were reassured a moment later, when the manager said:

"I think it will be a little more effective if Miss Alice makes her entrance from the other side. It brings her out better. Try it that way once, and then, if it goes, film it, Russ."

The benefit of the change was at once apparent, and after a moment of rehearsal it was decided on. Again the camera began its clicking and everyone breathed freely once more, Alice most of all, for failure would have meant so much to her.

"Very good - very good," spoke the manager encouragingly, as the play developed.

Alice and Ruth had rather difficult parts, and in one scene they held the stage alone, "plotting" to disclose the false count. It was in this scene that Alice had some effective work along comedy lines.

It seemed to go off very well - at least, as far as the girls could tell. Alice, as a rather hoydenish school girl, home for the summer, played havoc with the admirers of the romantic Ruth, who seemed to fill the role to perfection.

"You're doing well, little girl," whispered Paul to Alice, when she stepped out of the scene for a moment, while another part of the play went on.

"Do you really mean it?" she asked him.

"I certainly do. Say, you've got the other two guessing, all right."

"What other two?"

"Miss Pennington and Miss Dixon."

"Oh, I'm so sorry."

"Sorry for what?"

"I mean, I don't want them to dislike me," returned Alice.

"Oh, don't worry about that, little girl. They don't like anyone who can do better than themselves. But they're the only ones. The rest of us like you!"

"Really?"

"Well I should say!" and there was more energy in the words than was actually necessary. Alice blushed, but looked pleased.

"Very good!" observed the manager, after an effective scene in which Alice and Ruth took part. "You are doing excellent work. If this play is a hit I'll star you two in something more elaborate next week."

"Will you, really?" asked Ruth, as she came out of the scene.

"I really will," answered Mr. Pertell. "That's a promise!"

CHAPTER XVIII

A HIT

"Ruth, I do hope it's a success; don't you?" asked Alice.

"Of course I do. It means a whole lot."

"You mean to Mr. Pertell?"

"And to us, dear."

"What do you mean? Tell me."

The two girls were resting after the performance of the play "A False Count." The last scene had been filmed, and the long strips of celluloid, with the hidden pictures, sent to the dark room for development. Not until then could it be told whether the affair had been a success from a mechanical standpoint. And then, later, would come the test before the great public.

"Did you hear what Mr. Pertell said to me?" asked Ruth.

"Well, he said so much, directing us, and all that - I'm sure I don't recall anything special. What was it?"

"Why, he told me that if this play was a success - I mean if we showed up well in it - he'd give us parts in a big drama he's getting ready. Won't that be splendid?"

"Of course it will. But I liked this one very much. I wish I could see the real pictures."

"You can!" exclaimed a voice back of the girls, and, turning they saw Russ. "I'll take you to see them when the positives are made," he said.

"Oh, but I mean in a regular moving picture theater," went on Alice. "I'd like to see how the public takes us."

"I'll do that, too," agreed Russ. "As soon as the pictures are released we'll find some place where they are being shown, and you can watch yourself doing your act."

"That will be fine!" cried Ruth.

"What does 'released' mean?" asked Alice.

"Well, you know the moving picture business is something like the Associated Press," explained Russ. "The Associated Press is an organization for getting news. Often news has to be gotten in advance - say a thing like the President's message, or a speech by a big man.

"The Associated Press gets a copy in advance, and sends duplicates of it out to the newspapers that take its service. And on each duplicate copy is stamped a notice that it is to be released for publication on a certain day - or at even a certain hour. That is, it can't be used by the newspapers until that time.

"It's somewhat like that with moving pictures. The reels of new plays are sent out to the different theaters, and to fix it so a theater quite a distance from New York won't be at a disadvantage with one right here, which would get the film sooner, there is a certain date set for the release of the film. That means that though one theater gets it first it can't use it until the date set, when all the playhouses are supposed to have it."

"Oh, that's the way they do it?" observed Alice.

"Yes," went on Russ. "Of course the best stuff is what is called 'first run,'" he went on to explain. "That is, it is a reel of film of a new play, never before shown in a certain city. The best moving picture theaters take the first run, and pay good prices for it. Then, later on, second-rate theaters may get it at a lower price."

"And is our play a 'first run'?" asked Ruth.

"It will be for a time," answered Russ. "I think you girls did fine!" he went on. "Acting comes natural to you, I guess."

"Well, we've seen enough of it around the house, with daddy getting ready for some of his plays," admitted Alice. "Oh, I wish I could do it all over again!" she cried, gliding over to her sister and whirling her off in a little waltz to the tune of a piano that was playing so that the performers in another play, representing a ball room scene, might keep proper time.

"Did you like your part, Ruth?" asked Russ, after Alice had allowed her sister to quiet down.

"Yes. I always like a romantic character."

"I like fun!" confessed Alice. "The more the better!"

"Oh, will you ever grow up?" asked Ruth.

"I hope not - ever!" laughed Alice, gaily.

Off in another part of the studio Miss Pennington and her chum, Miss Dixon, were going through their parts. They looked over at Ruth, Alice and Russ, and their glances were far from friendly.

"I don't see what Mr. Pertell can see in those girls," remarked Miss Pennington, during a lull, when they did not have to be before the camera.

"Neither do I," agreed her friend. "They can't act, and the airs they put on!"

"Shocking!" commented Miss Pennington.

"Come, young ladies!" broke in the voice of the manager. "It is time for you to go on again. And please put a little more vim into your work. I want that play to be a snappy one."

"Humph!" sneered Miss Dixon.

"If he wants more snap he ought to pay more money," whispered her friend. "All he cares about now are those DeVere girls."

"Attention!" called the manager. "Get some good business into this, now. Mr. Switzer, when you come in, after that scene where you apply for work, and can't get it, you must throw yourself into your chair despondently. Do it as though you had lost all hope. You know what I mean."

"Vot you mean? Dot I should sit in it so?" and the German actor plumped himself into the chair in question by approaching it so that he could sit on it in astride, in reverse position, folding his arms over the rounded back.

"No - no, not that way - not as if you were riding a horse!" cried the manager. "Throw yourself into it with abandon, as the stage directions call for."

"Let me show him," broke in the melancholy voice of Wellington Bunn.

Striding into the scene, which had been interrupted to enable this bit of rehearsal to be gone through with, the old Shakespearean actor approached the chair and cast himself into it as though he had lost his last friend, and had no hope left on earth.

"That's the way - that's the idea - copy that!" cried Mr. Pertell, enthusiastically.

But he spoke too soon.

Mr. Bunn had cast himself into the chair with such "abandon" that the chair abandoned him. It fell apart, it disintegrated, it parted company with its legs - all at once - so that chair and actor came to the ground in a heap.

"Oh, my! I am injured! A physician, I beseech you!" moaned Mr. Bunn, while others of the cast rushed to help him to his feet. He was soon pulled from the ruins of the chair.

"Ach! So. I unterstandt now!" exclaimed Mr. Switzer. "I haf your meaning now, of vat 'abandon' is, Mr. Pertell. I am to break der chair ven I sits on it, yes? Dot is 'abandon' a chair. Vot a queer lanquitch der English is, alretty. Vell, brings me annuder chair und I vill abandon it!"

Mr. Pertell threw his hands upwards in a despairing gesture.

"No - no!" he cried. "I didn't mean that way."

"Than vot you means?" asked the German, puzzled.

Meanwhile Wellington Bunn was painfully walking over to a more substantial chair.

"That was all a trick!" he cried. "You did that on purpose, Mr. Snooks. You provided a broken chair!"

"I did not!" protested the property man. "It was the way you threw yourself into it. What did you think it was made of - iron?"

"I knew something would happen!" observed Mr. Sneed,

gloomily. "I felt it in my bones."

"Und I guess me dot he veels it in his bones, now," chuckled Mr. Switzer. "I am glat dot I, myself, did not abandon dot chair alretty yet."

The play went on after a little delay, and for some time after that the Shakespearean actor was very chary of offering to show other actors how to put "abandon" into their parts.

So far as could be told by an inspection of the negatives of the first important play in which Ruth and Alice had appeared, it was a success. Of course how it would "take" with the public was yet to be learned.

Meanwhile other plays were being considered, and Mr. Pertell repeated his promise, that if "A False Count" was successful he would give Ruth and Alice real "star" parts. They were eager for this, and, now that their father had seen how well they did, he was enthusiastic over them, and very glad to let them go on in the moving picture business.

"Who knows," he said, "but what it may mend the broken fortunes of the DeVere family?"

One evening Russ came over to the apartment of the girls.

"Come on out!" he called, gaily.

"Where?" asked Ruth.

"To the moving pictures. I've got a surprise for you. They are going to try my new invention for the first time."

"May we go, Daddy?" asked Alice, anxiously.

"Yes, I guess so," he answered, absentmindedly, hardly looking up from the manuscript of a new play he was studying.

So Russ took the girls.

"Oh, let's see what is going on!" begged Ruth, as they came to a halt outside a nearby moving picture theater.

"No, don't bother now!" urged Russ, gently urging them away from the lithographs and pictures in front of the place. "We're a bit late, and we want to get good seats."

He got them inside before they had more than a fleeting glimpse of the advertisements of the films that were to be shown, and soon they were comfortably settled.

"I wonder what we'll see?" mused Ruth, looking about the darkened theater. The performance was just about to start.

"I wish we could see our play," spoke Alice. "When do you think we can, Russ?"

"Oh, soon now," he answered, and the girls thought they heard him laugh. They wondered why.

The first film was shown - a western scene, and the girls were not much interested in it, except that Ruth remarked:

"The pictures seem much clearer than usual."

"That's on account of my invention," said Russ, proudly. "I'm glad you noticed it." Then the girls were more interested. A little later, when the title of the next play was shown, Ruth and Alice could not repress exclamations of pleased surprise. For it was "A False Count!"

"Why, Russ Dalwood!" whispered Alice. "Did you know this was here?"

"Sure!" he chuckled.

"Oh, that's why you hurried us in without giving us a chance to see what the bill was," reproached Ruth.

"Yes, I wanted to surprise you."

"Well, you did it all right," remarked Alice.

And then the girls gave themselves up to watching the moving pictures of themselves on the screen.

It was rather an uncanny experience at first, but they soon became used to it, and gave themselves up to the enjoyment of the little play, made doubly delightful from the fact that they had helped to make it.

"I'd hardly know myself," whispered Alice.

"Nor I," added her sister.

From the darkness behind them came a voice saying:

"I saw this play this afternoon, Mollie. It's fine. I like the tall actress best," and she referred to Ruth, whose presentment was then on the screen. "She's so romantic, I think."

"Listen to that!" Alice said to her sister. "Don't your ears burn?"

"Indeed they do. Oh! isn't it queer to see yourself, and hear yourself criticised?"

"Wasn't that fine?" demanded the unseen critic behind the sisters, as Ruth did an effective bit of acting. "Oh, I know I'm just going to love her. I hope she is in lots of films."

"So do I," added her companion. "But I like the small one best - the one that was in the scene before this."

"Oh, you mean the jolly one?"

"Yes."

"That's you, Alice," whispered Ruth. "Now it's your turn for your ears to burn."

"I thought you'd like this," commented Russ. "This film is a hit, all right."

And so it seemed, for the audience applauded when the little photo play was over, and that is a pretty good test.

"I think they were perfectly splendid," said another voice off to the left.

"Who, those two girls in that play?" some one asked.

"Yes. They're new ones, too. I haven't seen them in any of the Comet's other plays."

"Yes, I guess they must be new," and this was a girl's voice back in the darkness of the theater. "Oh, I'd like to meet them! I wish I could act for the movies!"

"She doesn't know how near she is to meeting us!" whispered Alice to her sister, as the next film was flashed on the white screen. "Did you ever have an experience like this before?"

"I never did!"

CHAPTER XIX

A BIT OF OUTDOORS

"Wasn't it fine!"

"Splendid! I never expected to see myself like that."

"Neither did I. Russ, how did you come to think of it?"

"Oh, it just came to me," he answered, chuckling.

The two "moving picture girls," as they laughingly called themselves, with Russ, were on their way home from the little theater where they had just witnessed the depiction of themselves on the screen. They had listened with amusement, not unmixed with pride, at the whispered comments on the play in which they had taken part.

"Do you think - I mean - would you call that a successful film, Russ?" asked Alice.

"I certainly would," he replied. "Didn't I take it myself?"

"That's so!" exclaimed Ruth. "But I wish Mr. Pertell could know how well it went. Not on our account," she added quickly, "but on account of his own business, and because dear daddy is in it. And the others, too - they'd be glad to know the audience liked it, I think."

"Don't worry," returned Russ. "Mr. Pertell will know it soon enough. He keeps track of all his films, and he knows which are successful or not. He'll hear of this one the first thing in the morning. The owners of the theaters where our films are used report as to which go the best. And their own re-orders also show that. So you'll be discovered, all right."

"Oh, it wasn't so much that!" declared Alice, quickly. "But it is new and strange to us, and I suppose we're too enthusiastic about it."

"Not a bit too enthusiastic!" Russ assured her. "That's what I like to see, and I guess the manager does, too. It would be a good thing if some of the others were a little more enthusiastic. They'd do better acting. Say!" he broke in, "what do you say to an ice cream soda? It's warm this evening," and he paused before a brilliantly lighted drug store.

"Shall we, Ruth?" asked Alice, with a queer little look at her sister.

"Oh, I don't know," began Ruth, hesitatingly.

"Which means - yes!" Alice cried, gaily. "Come on!"

Mr. DeVere looked up inquiringly from his bundle of manuscript as the girls and Russ entered the little apartment later.

"Oh, Daddy! It was just fine!" cried Alice, going over to him, and covering his eyes with her hands.

"We saw ourselves - and you, too, as others see us!" added Ruth.

"I - er - I don't understand," their father whispered.

"The moving pictures," explained Alice. "It was that play, 'A False Count,' you know. Oh, it made a great hit, I can tell you!"

"Ah, I'm glad to hear it," he said. "Sit down, Russ."

"No, I can't stay," answered the visitor from across the hall. "I've brought your daughters safely home, and now I have to get back. I've got a little work to do yet."

"Not at the studio; have you - so late?" asked Ruth.

"Oh, it isn't late," he laughed. "But I want to do a little work on my invention. I've sort of struck a snag, and it's bothering me. I want it as nearly perfect as I can get it, and I've thought of an improvement I can put on it. So I'll say good-night."

"Thank you, ever so much, for taking us!" said Alice, warmly.

"Yes, indeed, it was fine!" added Ruth, her eyes sparkling. "To think of seeing ourselves! It was a great surprise."

"Oh, you'll get used to it after a while," returned Russ. And then he went to his own room to labor ambitiously over his patent.

"No more work to-night, Dad!" announced Ruth, firmly, as she saw her father preparing to resume the study of the manuscript containing his part in a new moving picture drama. "Your eyes must be tired, and you must save them. It won't do to have them spoiled, as well as your voice."

"No, I suppose not," he answered, somewhat wearily. "This work is rather trying. I believe I would like to get out in the open for a change. Though I always said I never would do open-air parts in the movies."

"I'd like to get out, too," said Alice. "I enjoyed what little we did in the Brooklyn garden very much."

"I heard something at the studio about a prospect of the whole company being given a chance to do some outdoor dramas," observed Ruth, musingly. "I wonder what was meant?"

"Mr. Pertell will probably tell us when he has his plans perfected," Alice returned. "You know, though, that he promised if this 'A False Count' play should be a success he'd give us a chance in a more pretentious drama. I'm counting on that."

"And so am I," said Ruth. "Come, now, Daddy. No more work to-night."

As Russ had predicted, Mr. Pertell was not long in learning of the success of the play in which Ruth and Alice had main parts. In a day or so there came an increased demand for the films of the drama, and the manager was well pleased.

"And now I'm going to keep the promise I made you," he said to Ruth and Alice. "I've been holding back on a big drama, waiting until I saw how that one turned out. I didn't have any doubts, though, after I saw you two act. Now I'm going to star you in that. And afterward, well, we'll see what will happen. I've got a lot of ideas I want to try," he added.

"Mr. DeVere," the manager went on, "I believe you told me at one time that you did not care to do any acting that took you out in the open; am I right?"

"I did say that," admitted the actor, in his husky voice; "but I think I have changed my mind since then. I believe I would like to get out of doors more."

"Then I have the very thing for you and your daughters, too," the manager said. "That is, if they have no objection to going out of doors?" and he looked questioningly at them.

"We'd love it!" cried Alice.

"Then I'll make my plans," went on Mr. Pertell , after a

confirmatory nod from Mr. DeVere. "I think you'll like your parts. One of the acts takes place on a yacht. I've hired one for a little trip down the bay, and you can play at being millionaires for a day."

"How lovely!" cried Ruth, and clapped her hands gleefully.

"It is fine on the water these days!" exclaimed Alice.

"I'll have your parts ready soon," went on the manager. "I must start some of the other dramas going now," and he glanced about the studio. Off in one corner, talking together, were Miss Pennington and Miss Dixon, and, as the two actresses conversed they cast envious glances, from time to time, at Alice and Ruth. They were plainly jealous of the rapid rise of our two friends, but the moving picture girls bore in mind what motherly Mrs. Maguire had told them, and did not worry.

Mr. Pertell and his assistants gave out the parts in another play, and the rehearsals began. Almost at the start there was trouble.

"I'm not going to play that part!" objected Wellington Bunn, stalking with a tragic air toward the manager.

"Why, what's the matter with your part?"

"Why, you have been promising that you would put on one of Shakespeare's plays, and give me a chance in Hamlet, and here you go and cast me for one of a gang of counterfeiters. I have to wear a black mask. The public will not know that it is Wellington Bunn playing."

"Well, maybe it's a good thing they won't," murmured the manager, but what he said, aloud, was:

"You will have to take that part, Mr. Bunn, or look for another engagement."

"Then I'll leave!" the old actor declared gloomily.

But a little later he was observed to be putting on his mask, and taking his place in the "den of the counterfeiters," as the screen announced the place to be. It was one of the masterpieces of scenery evolved by Pop Snooks. And a little later he transformed the same scene, with a little manipulation, into the cave of a thirteenth century monk. Such was Pop Snooks.

"Ha! Ha! I haf a funny part!" laughed Carl Switzer, a little later.

"What is it?" asked Russ, who was getting a camera in readiness for action.

"Ha! It iss dot I go in a restaurant, und order a meal. Der vaiter he brings me some cheese und I am so thoughtfulness dot I put red pepper and horse radish on it. Den, ven I eat it I jumps ofer der table alretty yet. Dot is a fine part!" and he laughed gleefully, for Mr. Switzer was a simple soul.

A little later Alice and Ruth were given their new parts to study. It was announced that rehearsals would take place in a day or two, and many of the scenes were to be out of doors, some of them taking place on a yacht. Meanwhile Mr. DeVere went through with his role in a film drama, Ruth and Alice not being called on.

Finally announcement was made that the work of preparation for filming the big drama would be undertaken. This was the most ambitious play yet planned by Mr. Pertell, and he was anxious to make it a success.

That the price of success is high was amply proven in the next week. Everyone worked hard at the rehearsals, and none harder than Ruth and Alice. They were determined that their parts should be a credit to the performance. Later they learned that Miss Pennington and Miss Dixon had pleaded for the roles assigned to them.

But Mr. Pertell was true to his promise, and kept Alice and Ruth in their assigned places. The drama was an elaborate one, involving the making of special scenery, and Pop Snooks had to call in several assistants. But he liked that.

Then, too, the location of the outdoor scenes had to be chosen with care, to fit properly into the story.

But at last the rehearsals were complete, including those for the outdoor scenes. Of course the latter were rehearsed in the studio first, so that when the time came to film such as the scenes on the yacht, the pictures could be made without any preliminary trial on the vessel itself. To this end Pop had set up in the studio enough of the deck and fittings of a yacht to enable the performers to familiarize themselves with them.

"And now for the real thing!" exclaimed Russ, as a goodly part of the company, including Mr. DeVere and his daughters, started for the Battery one morning. They were to board the yacht there, and one of the scenes would show the girls going up the gang-plank.

It was a beautiful day in early summer, when even New York, with its rattle of elevated trains, rumble of the surface cars and hurry and scurry of automobiles, was attractive.

Quite a throng of curious people gathered when the film theatrical company prepared to board the vessel which had been chartered for the occasion. The embarking place was near the round building, now used as an Aquarium, but which, in former years, was Castle Garden, the immigrant landing station.

"All ready now - start aboard," ordered Mr. Pertell. "And, Russ, get your camera a little more this way. I want to show off the yacht as well as possible."

The moving picture operator shifted his three-legged machine to one side, and was about to start moving the film, as Ruth, Alice and the others, presumably of a gay yachting party, started up the gang-plank.

Several feet of film had been exposed, when there was a series of shouts and cries back of the crowd that had gathered to see the pictures made in the open air. Then came a warning:

"A runaway! A runaway horse! Look out!"

The crowd parted, and Ruth, looking up, saw a big horse, attached to a dray, dashing along one of the walks of Battery Park, having evidently come from one of the steamship piers nearby.

"Grab him, somebody!" yelled Mr. Pertell. "He'll spoil the picture!" That seemed to be his main thought.

On came the maddened animal, while the crowd scattered still more. Russ continued to make pictures, for the beast was not yet in focus.

"Go on! Keep moving!" directed Mr. Pertell to Ruth, Alice and the others. "Maybe you can get aboard before he gets here. Watch yourself, Russ!"

But the horse was charging directly for the gang-plank, and with frightened eyes Ruth, Alice and some of the others prepared to rush back to the pier.

"Go on! I'll get that horse!" cried a voice back of Mr. Pertell, and a man, apparently a farmer, sprang at the head of the plunging steed.

CHAPTER XX

FARMER SANDY APGAR

For a moment there was considerable confusion and excitement. Men in pursuit of the frantic animal had rushed after him, calling warnings to those in the zone of danger. Two policemen ran up to intercept the steed.

As for the moving picture actresses they hardly knew what to do. If the plunging animal crashed into the gang-plank he might injure a number of the performers, and break the rather frail structure, letting them slip into the water.

"That picture will be spoiled!" groaned Mr. Pertell.

"No, it won't!" cried Russ. "Go on! I'm getting you all right. The horse isn't in range yet and that young fellow has him now. Go on!"

Ruth and Alice gathered courage and the others followed, going through with the little gang-plank "business" called for in the play.

And indeed the quick-witted, rustic youth had the frantic horse in a firm grip. He seemed to know just how to handle frightened animals, and by the time the two policemen had reached him, the beast, though still restive, had quieted down.

"Good work, young fellow!" called one of the officers. "Whose horse is it?"

"I don't know, constable," was the answer, given with a country twang that caused several spectators to smile. "I jest seen him comin' and I see he was headed for them people what's goin' to Europe, I expect. I didn't want their voyage spoiled, so I jest jumped at his head."

"Well, you know how to do it, all right," said the second "constable," as the young farmer had called the policemen.

"I ought to know how to handle horses," was the answer, as the youth relinquished the reins to the officer. "I've been among 'em all my life. I was brought up on a farm."

He looked it, but there was something in his simple, manly face, and in the look of his honest blue eyes, that made one like him.

"Good work, all right!" repeated the first officer. "I'll take your name, young fellow, for my report," and he drew out a notebook. "I'll also want to find out to whom the horse belongs, but I s'pose the truckman's license number will be a clue."

"He's mine," broke in a voice, as a drayman pushed his way through the crowd. "Some boys got to fooling around him, and he started off. No damage done, I hope."

"No," replied the policeman, "but you want to tie your animal after this. He might have hurt someone - probably would have if it hadn't been for this chap. What's your name?" he asked the young farmer.

"Sandy Apgar."

"And where do you live?"

"On Oak Farm."

"Never heard of the place," went on the officer, with a smile.

"Oh, that's the name of our farm. It's jest outside the town of Beatonville, about forty miles back in Jersey."

"Oh, Jersey!" laughed the officer. "No wonder! Well, there's your horse, truckman. And now I want your name."

"Can I go, or do I have to appear in court?" asked Sandy Apgar. "I hope I don't, 'caused I'm in a hurry to git back to the farm. I've got a passel of work to do there, with the weather coming on the way it is.

"No, I guess you won't have to go to court," laughed the policeman. "We're much obliged to you."

"And so am I," added the truckman. "I haven't got any money to give you, because business is poor -"

"Oh, that's all right," said Sandy with a generous wave of his hand. "I don't stop runaway horses for a livin'. I farm it."

"If you ever want any carting done," went on the drayman, "you send for me, young feller, and it won't cost you a cent."

"Guess you wouldn't want to do any cartin' as far as Beatonville," laughed Sandy. "Folks out there don't ever move - they jest die and are buried in the same place. And I guess this is my last trip to New York in a long while. I'm jest as much obliged though," and patting the nose of the now quieted horse, he moved off through the thinning crowd. But he was not to escape unnoticed.

Mr. Pertell had learned, by a hasty talk with Russ, that the horse had been stopped just in time to avoid spoiling any of the film. Russ had continued to make the pictures and the first act of the new drama was a success. The other scenes would take place on board the chartered yacht.

So when the manager saw Sandy Apgar, who by his quick work had saved a film from being spoiled, making his way out of the throng, the theatrical man called to him:

"One moment, please. I want to thank you."

"Gosh! I'm getting thanked all around to-day!" laughed the young fellow.

"Well, I want to make it a little more substantial, then," went on the manager. "You saved me a few dollars."

"Oh, pshaw, that's nothing!" returned Sandy. "I guess your trip to Europe could have gone on."

"Europe?" questioned Mr. Pertell.

"Yes; ain't you folks going to Europe?"

"No, this is only a make-believe trip," laughed the manager. "It's for moving pictures. See, there's the chap who was taking the films, and they'd been spoiled if that horse got on the gang-plank. So you see what you did for us."

"Moving pictures; eh?" mused Sandy. "I thought they had to be took in the dark. Leastways, all I ever saw was in the dark."

"Oh, that's just to show them," the manager explained. "But we ought to be under way now. Can you come aboard for a little trip? We'll soon be back, and I want to thank you properly. I haven't time now. Come, take a little trip with us."

"Well, I s'pose I can," responded Sandy, slowly. "But I ought to be gettin' back to Oak Farm."

However, he went aboard the yacht, looking curiously about him, and more curiously at Russ, who began making more pictures as the yacht steamed off down the bay.

There were to be a number of scenes on board, but they would not be filmed until the yacht was farther out. Meanwhile, however, the progress of the ship down the bay was to be depicted on the screen, so Russ took pictures from either rail, no members of the company being required in these. Mr. Pertell thus had a chance to talk to Sandy.

The young fellow was very willing to tell about himself.

"Yes, I live on a farm," he said. "It's a right nice place, too, in summer, though lonesome in winter. I've lived there all my twenty-two years - never knew any other place."

"Do you live there all alone?" asked Ruth, for the young farmer had been introduced to the members of the company.

"No, my father and mother are there with me. Father is Mr. Felix Apgar - maybe you've heard of him?" the young man asked the manager, innocently.

"No, I don't think so," and Mr. Pertell had hard work to repress a smile.

"Well, he used to ship a lot of asparagus to New York, but maybe that was before your day," went on Sandy. "Pop is too feeble to work now, so I'm running the farm for him. And it - it's sorter hard," he added, rather pathetically. "Especially when you ain't got any too much money. I come to New York to raise some," he went on, "but folks don't seem to want to part with any - especially on a second mortgage."

"Is that what you came for?" asked Mr. Pertell.

"Yep. I come to raise some money - we need it bad, out our way, but I couldn't do it."

"Suppose you tell me," suggested Mr. Pertell. "I may be able to help you."

"Say, Mister, I reckon you've got enough troubles of your own, without bothering with mine," said Sandy. "Besides, maybe Pop wouldn't like me to tell. No, I'll jest make another try somewhere else. But we sure do need cash!"

"What for?" asked the manager, impulsively.

"Oh, maybe pop wouldn't like me to say. Never mind. It was sure good of you to ask me for this ride. The folks at Beatonville won't believe me when I tell 'em. But say, if ever you folks come out there, we'll give you a right good time - at Oak Farm!" he added, generously.

"Is your farm a large one?" asked the manager.

"Hundred and sixty acres. Some woodland, some flat, a lot of it hilly and stony, and part with a big creek on it."

"Hum," mused Mr. Pertell. "That sounds interesting. I've been looking for a good farm to stage several rural dramas on, and your place may be just what I need."

"To buy?" asked Sandy, eagerly.

"Oh, no. But I might rent part of it for a time. I'll talk to you about it later. I've got to get some of these scenes going now," and the manager went to confer with Russ.

CHAPTER XXI

OVERHEARD

The trip down the bay on the yacht was enjoyed by all, even though much of the time was taken up in depicting scenes from the drama. Sandy Apgar looked on curiously while the drama was being filmed, and when Ruth and Alice were not acting they talked to the young farmer.

They found him good-natured and rather simple, yet with a fund of homely wit and philosophy that stood him in good stead. He described Beatonville to them, and the farm where he and his aged parents tried to wrest a living from nature - that was none too kind.

"I've had quite a little vacation since I come to New York," Sandy said, "though it did take quite a bit of money. I reckon pop, though, will be disappointed that I can't bring back with me the promise of some cash."

"Then you need money very badly?" asked Alice.

"Yes, Miss. And I guess there ain't many farmers but what do. Leastways, I never met any that was millionaires. Though if the folks back home could see me now they'd think I was one, sittin' here doin' nothin'. It sure is great!"

The girls were called away to enact some of the scenes requiring their presence, and when they came back they found

Sandy in conversation with the manager.

The girls saw Mr. Pertell give Sandy some bills, and when the young farmer protested, the manager said:

"Now never mind that!! You saved me more than that in stopping that runaway horse from spoiling my film and scene. You just take it, and when I get a chance I'll run up to your farm and look it over.

"I haven't got all my plans made yet, but I'm thinking of making a series of plays with an old-fashioned farm as a background. Is your place old-fashioned?" he asked.

"That's what some city folks said once, when they stopped in their automobile to get a glass of milk," replied Sandy. "We haven't any electric lights, nor even a telephone. So I guess we're old-fashioned, all right."

"I should say so," laughed Mr. Pertell. "Well, it may be the very thing I need when I go out on the rural circuit with my company. If it is, I could pay for the use of your farm, and it wouldn't interfere with your getting in the crops. In fact, I would probably want some scenes of harvesting, and the like."

"Well, come and we'll make you welcome," responded Sandy, warmly. "Only I never expected to get paid for stopping a runaway horse," he added as he looked at the roll of bills.

"Well, take it and have a good time during the rest of your stay in New York," advised the manager.

"Money's too scarce to waste on a good time," replied the young farmer, cautiously. "I'll use this to make up what I spent on railroad fare. My trip was a failure, but pop and mom will be glad it didn't cost me as much as I calculated, thanks to you. I hope you will get out to Oak Farm."

"Oh, you'll probably see me," Mr. Pertell assured him. "Give me your address."

The making of the films went on, and the water scenes of this latest and most elaborate drama were nearly all taken.

"Now we will have the scene in the small boat, where the party puts off to visit friends on the other vessel," announced Mr. Pertell. "They don't actually get there, as the alarm on board this vessel brings them back. But we'll have to show the start. Now, Mr. Sneed, you are to go in the small boat first."

Some of the sailors on board the yacht prepared to lower a boat from the davits, but Pepper Sneed held back.

"Do I have to get into that small boat?" he asked, dubiously.

"Certainly!" replied Mr. Pertell. "There is no danger."

"No danger!" cried Pepper Sneed. "What! In that small boat? Look at the waves!" and he pointed over the side. There was only a gentle swell on.

"It's as calm as a mill pond," spoke one of the sailors.

"Mill pond! Don't say mill pond to me!" cried the grouchy actor. "I fell in one once."

"Well, you won't fall now," declared the manager. "Get in the boat. I
want to show it being lowered over the side with you in it."

"Well, if I have to - I'll have to, I suppose," groaned Mr. Sneed. "But I know something will happen."

But matters seemed going smoothly enough. The sailors were carefully lowering the small craft, and it was nearly at the surface of the water. Russ, up in the bow of the yacht, where he could get a good view, was making the pictures.

Suddenly, when the boat was a few feet from the ripples on the bay, one of the ropes slipped quickly through the davit block. One end of the boat went down quite fast and Pepper Sneed was heard to yell:

"Here I go! I knew something would happen! Help! I'm going to sink! Help! Oh, why did I ever get into this business!"

But with great presence of mind the other sailors lowered away on their rope, so that the other end of the boat went down also, and in another instant it was riding on an even keel. Nothing had happened except that Pepper Sneed had been badly scared.

"Did you get that, Russ?" asked the manager, anxiously.

"Oh, yes."

"How was it?"

"Fine! It will be all the better with that little mistake in - look more natural."

"Good! Then we'll leave it in. Now the rest of you get down the accommodation ladder. Stay there, Mr. Sneed!" he called to the grouchy actor, who seemed to want to leave the boat.

"What! Are more of them coming in this little cockleshell?"

"Certainly. That boat will hold twenty. Keep your place."

"Well, we'll all be drowned, you mark my words!" predicted Mr. Sneed. But nothing else happened and that part of the film was successfully made.

Then came more scenes aboard the yacht, until the water parts of the drama were completed.

Late that afternoon the party of moving picture players

returned to New York. Sandy Apgar bade his new friends good-bye, expressing the hope that he would soon see them at Oak Farm.

"Excuse me, Mr. Pertell," said Alice, when they got back to the studio, and instructions had been given out for the indoor rehearsals next day, "excuse me, but I could not help overhearing what you said about the possibility of some farm dramas. Do you intend to film some of those?"

"Indeed I do," he answered, with a smile. "Why, would you and your sister like to be in them?"

"Very much!"

"Well, then, if this big play proves a success - and I see no reason why it should not - I shall take you and the rest of the company out to the country for the summer. We may go to Oak Farm, or to some other place; but we'll try a circuit of rural dramas, and see how they go."

Alice went to tell Ruth the good news. She found her sister in the dressing room, getting ready for the street.

"I think that will be fine!" exclaimed Ruth. "Listen, dear, daddy told me he had some business to attend to downtown, so he won't be home to supper. He suggested that we two go to a restaurant, and I think I'd like it - don't you? It will round out the day!"

"Of course. Let's go. I'm *so* hungry from that little water trip!"

A short time afterward the girls sat in a quiet restaurant, not far from the moving picture studio. There were not many persons there yet, for it was rather early. Ruth and Alice had taken a cosy little corner, of which there were a number in the place.

"We are coming on!" remarked Alice, as she gave her order.

"We certainly are!" agreed Ruth. "Who would ever have thought that we would get to be moving picture girls? I think -"

"Hush!" cautioned Alice, raising her hand for silence. Then the two girls heard some men in the next screened-off place talking, and one of them spoke loudly enough to be overheard.

"I'm sure we can get it," he was saying. "It's a nice little patent, and all the movies in the country will want it. It makes the pictures clearer and steadier. I tried to make a deal with him for it, but he turned me down. Now I'm going to get it anyhow, if you'll help."

"But how can you get it if it's patented?" another voice asked.

"That's the joke of it. It isn't patented yet. And all we need is the working model, and we can make one like it and patent it ourselves. Are you with me?"

"I guess so - yes!" was the answer.

"Good, then we'll get the model to-night and start a patent of our own. I know where he's taken it."

There was a scraping of chairs, indicating that the men were leaving. Ruth and Alice gazed at each other with startled eyes.

CHAPTER XXII

THE WARNING

"Did you hear that?" asked Ruth of Alice, in a whisper.

"Yes! Hush! Don't let them hear you!"

Ruth looked apprehensively over the back of her chair, but beheld no one. The noise made by the men as they were going out grew fainter.

Alice rose from her chair.

"What are you going to do?" asked Ruth, laying a detaining hand on her sister's arm.

"I'm going to see who those men are."

"Don't. They may -"

Alice made a gesture of silence.

"I'm pretty sure who one of them is," she whispered, as she bent down close to Ruth. "But I want to make certain."

"But Alice -"

"Now, Ruth, be sensible," went on Alice, as she passed around back of her sister's chair. "You heard what was said. I'm sure those men have some designs on that patent Russ has worked so hard over. We must tell him about them, and put him on his guard."

"You may get into danger."

It was curious how, in this emergency - as she had often done of late - Alice took the lead over her older sister. And Ruth did not object to it, but seemed to follow naturally after Alice led the way.

"Danger!" laughed Alice softly, as she came to a position behind the screen, whence she could note who the men going out were. "There's no danger in a public restaurant like this. And I'm only going to make sure who that man is. Then we'll go tell Russ."

Ruth made no further objection, and turned to watch her sister. The men had come to a halt at the desk of the cashier, to pay their checks, and their backs were toward Alice. An instant later, however, one of them had turned around and faced toward the rear of the restaurant.

Alice darted behind the screen with a quick intaking of her breath. She had recognized the man, and was fearful lest he know her.

For he was the fellow with whom Russ had been in dispute in the hallway that day, when the DeVeres' door had flown open.

"Simp Wolley!" whispered Alice, in tense tones to Ruth. "It's that man who was after Russ's patent."

"Then don't let him see you."

"I won't - no danger. They're going out now. Come on!"

"Where?" asked Ruth, as Alice reached for her gloves.

"We must go to warn Russ."

"But we haven't eaten what we ordered," objected Ruth, pointing to the food, hardly touched, on the table.

"No matter, we can pay for it."

"But the cashier will think it so odd."

"What do we care. It's our food - we'll pay for it, and we can do what we like with it then. We can eat it or not."

"But they'll think it so queer. They may think we have some prejudice against it, and -"

Ruth was a stickler for the established order of things. Alice was more in the habit of taking "cross-cuts."

"Don't be silly!" exclaimed the younger girl. "We've just got to get out of here and warn Russ before those men have a chance to take his patent. You heard what they said about doing it to-night!"

"Well, I suppose we must," assented Ruth, with a sigh. "But it seems a shame to waste all that good food."

"It won't be wasted. We can tell them to give it to some poor person."

"Oh, Alice! You are so - so queer."

"I'd be worse than queer if I sat here and ate while Russ was being robbed of his patent. I should think you'd want to help him. I thought you and he -"

"Alice!" warned Ruth, with a sudden assumption of dignity. But she blushed prettily.

"Oh, you know what I mean. Come on. Don't sit there talking

any longer, and raising objections. We've got to hurry."

"Yes, I suppose so. Oh, Alice, I hope nothing happens!"

"So do I."

"I mean to us."

"And I mean to Russ. A distinction without a difference."

The two girls drew on their gloves and left the restaurant. As Ruth had expected, the cashier at the desk looked at them curiously as they paid for the meal they had not eaten. But Alice forestalled any open criticism by saying:

"We find we have to leave sooner than we expected. If you like, give our meal to some poor person. We haven't had time to touch it."

"Oh, all right," answered the young girl at the desk. "We often give what is left over to charity, and I'm sure the food on your table won't come amiss. If you like I'll speak to the manager, and see if he'll give you a rebate -"

"No, we haven't time for that - too much of a hurry," answered Alice. "Come along, Ruth."

They hurried outside, and Alice glanced quickly up and down the street for a glimpse of the two men. They were not in sight.

"I wish we were rich!" suddenly exclaimed Alice, as she took her sister's arm, and hurried in the direction of the elevated that would take them home.

"Why?" asked Ruth.

"Because then we could afford to take a taxicab. We ought to warn Russ as soon as possible. How much money have you, Ruth?"

"Not enough for a taxicab, I'm afraid." She hastily counted it over. Alice did the same.

"No," decided the younger girl, with a sigh. "I guess we'd better not. At least - not yet. We may have to - later."

"What do you mean?" asked Ruth.

"I mean we can't tell what will happen before we are able to tell Russ. He's hardly likely to be at home now, and we may have to search for him."

"But we can go home and tell his mother and Billy. One of them could find him, and warn him. Billy knows New York even better than we do."

"Yes, I suppose so. Well, we'll go to the apartment and see what happens there."

But at the Fenmore the girls had their first disappointment, for none of the Dalwoods was at home. Nor did any of the neighbors know where they had gone. For persons in New York, even in the same apartment house, are not very likely to become acquainted with one another, and often families may live in adjoining flats for a long time, without passing beyond the bowing stage. As for keeping track of the comings and goings of their neighbors, it is never thought of, unless something out of the ordinary occurs.

Echoes only answered the knocking of Ruth and Alice, and the two girls faced each other in the hallway with anxious looks on their faces.

"What shall we do?" asked Ruth. "None of them is home. How can we warn Russ?"

"I don't know. I've got to think!" exclaimed Alice. "Come in our place and let's sit down a minute. We can make a cup of tea. I was so hungry, and to leave that nice little meal - well, we just had to do it, that's all."

Tea was soon in process of making, and while the girls set out some cakes and a jar of jam for a hasty meal they did some rapid thinking.

"Did you ever hear Russ say where it was he was having his patent attachment made?" asked Alice.

"I never did," confessed Ruth. "He said it was somewhere on the East Side, but that's very indefinite."

"Then the only thing to do is to find Russ and tell him," decided Alice, as she removed, with the tip of her tongue, a spot of jam from a forefinger. "We've just got to find him.

"Now I'll tell you what we'll do, Ruth. You stay here and as soon as Mrs. Dalwood, or Billy, or perhaps even Russ comes home, you tell them all about this plot."

"But what will you do?"

"I'll go find Russ."

"What! Alone?"

"Why not? We can't both go. Oh, I see!" and a light broke over the face of Alice. "You mean you think it's *your* place to warn him. Well, maybe it is. I'm sure he would like -"

"Now, Alice, I didn't mean that at all, and you know it. I meant you oughtn't to be going about New York alone, and it's getting late. It will soon be dark."

"Nonsense! It isn't six o'clock yet."

"I know. But I can't allow you. We'll both go."

"But someone ought to be here to tell them as soon as one

comes home."

"We can write a note and leave it under the door. Then we can leave a note for daddy. He'll be worried when he comes back and finds us gone. That's the best plan, Alice. Leave a note for Russ, and then you and I will try to find him. They may know at the studio where he has gone. Or he may be there yet."

"All right!" agreed Alice, after a moment's thought.

CHAPTER XXIII

THE MISSING MODEL

Two notes were quickly written. One was left on the table in the girls' apartment, telling their father that they were going out for a little while, to try to locate Russ on a matter of some importance connected with the moving pictures.

"There's no use telling daddy what has happened," said Alice. "He would only worry, and really there's no danger. We are merely going to warn Russ. He'll have to look after the men himself. But daddy would be sure to think we would get into some trouble. So we may as well not bother him."

"All right!" agreed Ruth. She was entering into the spirit of the affair now. Her eyes were shining and her cheeks vied in hue with those of Alice.

The other note, marked "Urgent!" was thrust under the kitchen door of the Dalwood flat.

"They'll be sure to see that," remarked Alice. "And, no matter if only Billy comes home first, he'll know what to do," for the story of the men's talk in the restaurant had been briefly set down on the paper.

Then, but not without many misgivings, the girls set out to try to find Russ.

"We can call up the studio on the telephone," suggested Alice, as she and her sister reached the street. "That will be the quickest way. If Russ isn't there they may be able to tell us where he is, or Mr. Pertell may know where the model is - I mean the machine shop where the apparatus is being turned out."

"That's so," agreed Ruth. "Why, we could have used one of the telephones in the apartment!"

"No, some of the neighbors would overhear us, and we don't want that."

"Why not?" Ruth wanted to know.

"Because you can't tell but one of those men may be watching this place, and some of the neighbors may be in league with them. Besides, all the telephones here are on party wires, and when you talk over one, some of the other subscribers on the same circuit may listen, for all we can tell. It isn't safe."

"My! You think of everything!" exclaimed Ruth, admiringly. "How do you manage it?"

"Oh, it just seems to come to me," replied Alice, with a laugh. "Come on," she added, after they had walked a little way. "There's a drug store and there's a telephone booth in it. Do you want to talk to Russ, in case he's there?"

"Oh, no, you'd better," responded Ruth, blushing.

"I will not. I'll call up the studio, but if he's there I want you to be the one to tell him. He'll appreciate it."

"All right," agreed Ruth, and the blush grew deeper.

Alice quickly got the number of the moving picture studio. There was a private branch exchange there, and Alice knew the girl operator.

"I want to get Russ Dalwood in a hurry," Alice explained to Miss Miller, who ran the switchboard. "You try the different departments until you find him. I'll be here, holding the wire."

"All right!" returned Miss Miller, in crisp, business-like tones. Perhaps she suspected that something was wrong.

Then ensued a nervous waiting. Alice opened the door of the booth and told Ruth what she had done.

"I'll let you talk to Russ as soon as he answers," she said.

Ruth nodded understandingly. But it seemed that Russ was not to be so easily found. Through her receiver Alice could hear Miss Miller ringing the telephones in the different departments of the big studio building. One after the other was tried, from the office to the dark developing rooms, and then the printing rooms. Most of the employees had gone for the day, but such as were present evidently made answer that the young moving picture operator was not there.

"I can't locate him," said Miss Miller to Alice, finally. "They say he was here about a half-hour ago, but has gone out."

"Don't they know where he went?" asked Alice. "It's very important that we find him."

"I'll see if anyone knows," came back the answer. Then ensued more waiting, but at the end came a gleam of hope.

"Mr. Blackson, in the camera room, says he heard Russ say he was going to the Odeon Theater," Miss Miller stated. "He is trying to get one of his attachments tried there."

"Where is the Odeon?" asked Alice, nervously drumming with her fingers on the telephone shelf.

"It's on Eightieth Street somewhere. Wait, I'll look up the telephone number for you. They take our service, you know."

In a few seconds Miss Miller had given the desired information, and then Alice said "good-bye" to her, frantically working the receiver hook of her instrument up and down to call the attention of the main central operator.

"And give them a good, long ring!" Alice added, as she gave the number. "It's very important."

"Very well," answered central.

There came more waiting. It was a bad time to get anyone, for it was now shortly after six o'clock, just when most persons were leaving for home or supper.

"Can't you get them?" asked Ruth, as Alice opened the 'phone booth door for a breath of air.

"I'm trying, dear. He'd left the studio, but may be at a moving picture theater. There, they've answered at last!"

Alice pulled the door shut with her disengaged hand, and spoke eagerly into the transmitter.

"Is Mr. Russ Dalwood there? It's very important!"

Ruth saw the look of dismay that came over her sister's face. Then through the double glass door she heard Alice say:

"He's gone! And you don't know where? Left ten minutes ago? Oh dear!"

Slowly she hung up the receiver. There seemed nothing else to do. She came out of the booth, her face showing her disappointment.

"He's gone, Ruth," she said. "What had we better do?"

"I think the only thing to do is to go back home and wait for him. He may be there now. Or his mother or Billy may. Come on home."

It was Ruth who was directing now, and Alice, after a moment of thought, saw that this was the only thing to do. Quickly they retraced their steps to the apartment house. Without stopping to enter their own flat they knocked on the Dalwood door. A few seconds of anxious waiting brought no answer.

"Not home yet!" exclaimed Alice. "Oh, what a shame."

Ruth turned to their own flat. Entering with a pass-key she saw at a glance that their father had not come home. The note for him was still on the table.

Then, as puzzled and disappointed, the two girls stood in the center of the room, they heard someone coming up the stairs that led to their flat. A second later and a merry whistle broke out.

"There he is - that's Russ!" cried Alice, joyfully. "I'll tell him; no - you go!" she added hastily, thrusting her sister before her into the hallway.

The whistle broke off into a discord as Russ saw Ruth standing waiting for him. Something in her face must have told him something was the matter, for he came up the remaining steps three at a time.

"What is it? What has happened?" he asked. "Is someone hurt?"

"No, it's your patent - the model. Some men - Alice and I overheard them in the restaurant - we've been trying to get you on the 'phone - I - we -"

Then Alice broke in.

"They're after your moving picture machine patent, Russ! They're going to get it to-night - Simp Wolley! You've got to hurry!"

Between them the girls quickly told what they had overheard.

Russ's eyes snapped.

"So that's the game; is it?" he cried. "Well, I'll stop them! I'm mighty glad you told me. My patent model, the drawings and everything are at Burton's machine shop. It isn't far from here. I'll go right away - in a taxicab. Do you -" he hesitated a moment. "Do you want to come?"

"We might be able to help," suggested Alice to Ruth. "At any rate, we'll have to give evidence against those men if they get them. Shall we go, Ruth?"

"I - I think so - yes."

"Bravo!" whispered Alice in her ear. "That note to daddy will answer. You'd better leave another in place of the one we wrote to you, Russ."

"I will," he exclaimed as he entered his own flat. "But mother and Billy won't be home until late, anyhow. They're going to stay to supper with relatives. Still, I'll explain in case I should be delayed."

Quickly he dashed off another note for his mother, and then, with the two girls, he hurried down to the street. There was a taxicab stand just around the corner, and the three were quickly on their way to the machine shop, while Ruth and Alice took turns giving more details of the scene in the restaurant.

"Here we are!" announced Russ, a little later, as the cab drew up, with a screeching of brakes, in front of a rather dingy building. "I only hope we're in time, and that Burton hasn't gone yet."

He jumped out of the cab, leaving Ruth and Alice sitting there. Frantically he threw open the door and rushed up the shop stairs.

"Oh, I do hope he is in time," breathed Ruth, softly.

"So do I," spoke Alice. "I wonder how men can be so mean as to want to take what isn't theirs?"

"I don't know, dear. Oh, hasn't this been an exciting day?"

"I should say it had. If ever - there's Russ now!" she interrupted herself to exclaim. "Oh, Ruth. It looks as though we were too late!"

For Russ, with a dejected look on his face, was crossing the pavement toward the cab.

"It - it's gone," he said brokenly. "Simp Wolley was here a half-hour ago and got it!"

"But how could he?" asked Alice in surprise. "Who gave it to him?"

"Mr. Burton. There was a forged order, supposed to be from me, and the machinist handed over the model," and Russ extended a crumpled and grimy bit of paper.

CHAPTER XXIV

THE PURSUIT

"How did it happen, Russ?"

"Where have the men gone with the model?"

"Can't you get some trace of them?"

Thus Ruth and Alice questioned their friend, as he stood at the open window of the taxicab, looking at the crumpled paper.

"I - I don't understand it all," he confessed. "After I knew those fellows were after my patent I cautioned Mr. Burton about letting any strangers see it."

A figure came into the doorway of the machine shop. It was that of an elderly man, with steel-rimmed spectacles. His face was grimy with the dirt of metal.

"I'm awfully sorry, Russ," he said, contritely. "But of course I thought the note was from you, and gave up the model."

"Did Simp Wolley get it?" asked Alice, eagerly.

"No, a uniformed messenger boy came for it," explained Russ. "That was it; wasn't it, Mr. Burton?"

"Yes. And I had no suspicions. You know you had said you

might want the model some time in a hurry, to demonstrate to possible buyers, and of course when the boy came with the note I supposed you had sent him. I'm not familiar enough with your handwriting to know it," he added.

"No, I suppose not," admitted Russ. "And yet if you had been this might have deceived you. It is very like my writing. I guess Wolley must have had a sample to practice on."

"It all seemed regular," went on Mr. Burton. "I was working away, making some of the finished appliances from your model and drawings, when the boy brought the note. He was a regular messenger boy, I could tell that. And the note only asked for the model - not for any of the finished machines, of which I had two. He didn't even want the drawings, or I might have been suspicious."

"They won't need the drawings as long as they have the model. They can make drawings themselves," spoke Russ.

"But if they only have the model, and you still have some of the finished appliances," asked Alice, "can't you get ahead of them yet?"

"I'm afraid not," Russ replied. "You see, the patent office doesn't require models to be filed in all cases now. You can get a patent merely on drawings. They can still get ahead of me."

"Not if you file your drawings now!" exclaimed Ruth.

"Yes, but I'm not ready. You see the machine isn't perfected yet. I am still working on it. But they can file a prior claim, and get a patent on something so near like mine that I would be refused a patent when I applied.

"You see I haven't made any formal application yet. Of course, if it came to a question of a lawsuit, I might beat them out. But I have no money to hire lawyers, and they have. The only thing for me to do is to get that model back before they have a chance to use it to make drawings from. And how to do it I don't know."

"Do you know who that messenger boy was?" asked Alice suddenly of the machinist.

"I never saw him before, Miss - no. He came in a taxicab."

"A taxicab!" cried Russ, excitedly. "You didn't say that before. Did you happen to notice the number?"

If ever Russ Dalwood was thankful it was then, and the cause of it was that Mr. Burton had a mathematical mind in which figures seemed to sprout by second nature.

"I did notice the number," he said. "It isn't often that taxicabs stop out in front here, and I looked from my window as one drew up at the curb. I was working on your patent at the time. I saw the number of the cab, later, as the messenger boy rode off in it with the model."

"What was it?" asked Russ, preparing to make a note.

The machinist gave it to him.

"Now if we can only trace it!" exclaimed the young inventor.

"I guess I can help you out, friend," broke in their own taxicab chauffeur. "I've got a list of all the cabs in New York, and the companies that run them." Rapidly he consulted a notebook, and soon had the desired information. The office of the company was not far away, and Russ and the girls were soon speeding toward it. What the next move was to be no one could say.

The manager remembered the call that had come in. Two men had come with a messenger boy to engage a cab to go to the address of the machine shop.

"And who were the two men?" asked Russ.

The manager described one whom Ruth and Alice had no difficulty in recognizing as Simp Wolley.

"The other man was shorter and not so well dressed," the cab manager went on.

"Bud Brisket!" exclaimed Russ. "I know him. Now the question is: Where did they take my model?"

"There I'm afraid I can't help you," said the manager.

"Wait!" exclaimed Alice. "Did you happen to notice the number on the messenger boy's cap?"

"No, I did not, I'm sorry to say," the man answered.

"Then that clue is no good," spoke Russ, with a sigh.

"It might be," put in Ruth. "The messenger was probably engaged from the office nearest here. We could find that and make some inquiries."

"So we could!" cried Alice. "Oh, Ruth, you're a dear!"

Russ looked as though he would have said the same thing had he dared.

An inquiry over the telephone to the main office of the messenger service, brought the desired information. And soon, in their taxicab Russ, Ruth and Alice were at the sub-station. There the identity of the messenger was soon learned, and he was sent for.

"Sure, I went to de machine shop," admitted the snub-nosed, freckled-faced lad. "I got some sort of a thing. I didn't know what it was."

"And where did you take it?" asked Russ eagerly.

"Right where dem men told me to. Dey met me around de corner, got in de cab and rode off wid it."

"And what did you do?" asked the manager of the messenger.

"Oh, dey gave me carfare, an' a tip, and I come back here."

"But where did they go?" asked Russ.

"Off in de taxi. I didn't notice."

Russ looked hopeless, but Ruth exclaimed:

"We've got to go back to the taxi office and see the chauffeur of that car. He's the only one who can tell us where the men are."

"Good!" cried Russ. "We'll do it."

Back again they went, to find that the car had just come in, after a long trip. The chauffeur readily gave the address to which he had driven the two men, after the messenger boy had gotten out. It was in an obscure section of Jersey City.

"And there's where I'm going!" cried Russ. "Wolley and Brisket are probably going to try to work their scheme from there. But maybe I can stop them."

"I - I think we had better go home, Alice dear," said Ruth gently, at this point.

"Yes," sighed the other, "though I'd love to be there at the finish!"

"Alice!" gasped her sister.

"Well, I would," she said, defiantly.

"Maybe it wouldn't be best," suggested Russ. "I'll get a friend of mine, though. Now shall I take you home?"

"No, indeed!" cried Ruth. "That will delay you. You go right on after them. Alice and I can get home all right. It isn't late."

"It will give me pleasure if the young ladies will allow me to send them home in one of our cabs," put in the manager. "I am sorry that any of our men was used in a criminal manner."

"It wasn't your fault," spoke Russ. "But I guess the girls will be glad to be sent home. I'll keep on. I haven't any time to lose."

And while he sped off in his taxi, in pursuit of the men who were trying to cheat him out of his patent, Ruth and Alice took their places in another cab, and were driven back to the Fenmore Apartment.

CHAPTER XXV

THE CAPTURE

Mr. DeVere was rather worried when he reached home, and found his daughters' note. He puzzled over what could have taken them out with Russ, and went across the hall to inquire. By this time Mrs. Dalwood had returned, and found the note her son had left.

There was not much information in it - Russ had not had time for that - and the mystery seemed all the deeper.

"I wonder what I had better do?" asked Mr. DeVere of Mrs. Dalwood.

"Just don't do anything - and don't worry," she advised. "I know your daughters are able to take care of themselves - especially Miss Alice."

"Yes, she seems very capable - of late," he agreed, remembering how she had worked to get him into the moving picture business.

"And with Russ no harm will come to them," went on Mrs. Dalwood. "He's a good boy."

"Indeed he is! But I wish I knew what it was all about."

There was the honk of an auto horn in the street below, and as they looked out, they saw, in the gleam of a street lamp, Ruth and Alice alighting.

"There they are now!" exclaimed Mr. DeVere, with a note of relief in his voice.

"But Russ isn't with them!" said Mrs. Dalwood, in surprise. "I wonder what can have happened to him?"

Anxiously the two parents waited until the girls came up.

"Oh, such a time!" cried Alice, breathlessly.

"Where's Russ?" demanded his mother.

"After the men - Simp Wolley and Bud Brisket!"

"Oh, those horrid men!"

"He's all right," said Ruth, gently. "He is going to get Mr. Pertell and an officer to go with him."

"But what is it all about?" asked Mr. DeVere.

Then, rather disjointedly, and with many interruptions, the girls told the story of the afternoon and evening, for it was now nearly nine o'clock. Of course Mr. DeVere and Mrs. Dalwood were much worried when they learned what had happened, and the widow was not at her ease when she thought of her son still not out of danger.

"But I'm sure he will soon be back," declared Alice, confidently. She was a great comfort in trouble - a real optimist.

Then followed a period of anxious waiting.

It was broken by the return of Russ, rather disheveled, tired and excited, but with his precious model safe in the taxicab with him and Mr. Pertell.

"Why, Russ, where have you been?" cried Mrs. Dalwood.

"I just wish I'd been there!" exclaimed Billy. "Was there a fight, Russ?"

"A - little one," he admitted, with a glance at the girls. "But it was soon over."

"And where are the men now?" asked Alice.

"Safe in jail."

Then he told what had happened.

After Alice and Ruth had gone home in the taxicab he had called for Mr. Pertell, explaining what had occurred. A special officer was engaged, and the three went to the address in Jersey City, where Wolley and Brisket had gone with the model. The place was in a rather disreputable neighborhood. In a back room, which was approached with caution, the two plotters were found with a draughtsman whom they had hired to make drawings of the model.

The two scoundrels were taken by surprise and easily overpowered, after a short resistance. The draughtsman was an innocent party, and was allowed to go, after promising to give evidence against Wolley and Brisket. The latter were put under arrest, and with his precious model safe in his possession Russ started for home.

"They didn't have time to do a thing!" exclaimed the young inventor, enthusiastically. "Thanks to you girls."

"Oh, we didn't do anything," said Ruth, modestly.

"I think you did!" cried Russ, looking at her admiringly.

"It was all Alice!" she said.

"'Twas you who thought of the most practical plans!" insisted the younger girl. "Oh, Russ! I'm so glad!"

"And so am I," said Ruth, softly.

"Well, I must say, for two girls who haven't been much in public life, you two are coming on," said Mr. DeVere, in his hoarse tones. "But I am glad of it!"

The prompt action of Alice and Ruth, enabling Russ to recover his invention, worked against the plans of the plotters. They were easily convicted of fraud, and sent to prison. As for the invention of Russ, he soon perfected it, and put it out on royalty. Many moving picture machine men agreed to use it on their projectors, and to pay him a sum each year for the privilege. So Russ was assured of a goodly income for some time.

* * * * *

"Well," said Ruth the next morning, as she and Alice arose late after their evening of excitement, "now that is over, the next matter to be considered is: What are we going to do from now on?"

"Act in moving pictures, I should say," replied Alice. "We seem to be committed to it now. I wonder how that big drama came out? I hope it's a success. For I do so want to go on the rural circuit; don't you?"

"I think I do," answered Ruth.

"Russ is going along to make the pictures, I believe," added Alice, softly.

"Is he?" asked Ruth, with an air of indifference. "And I suppose Paul Ardite will be one of the company," she added.

"How'd you guess?" laughed Alice.

"A little bird told me."

Two days later the entire company who had taken part in the making of the big film, scenes of which were laid on the yacht, were invited to see the pictures projected.

From the very first it was seen that the play was going to be a success - at least from a mechanical standpoint and some time later it was demonstrated to be a success from a popular one also.

The girls looked on while the pictures of themselves, their father and others of the company were thrown on the white screen. They saw the scene at the gang-plank, where the runaway had almost spoiled it, but there was no sign of the horse in the pictures. Sandy Apgar had taken care of that.

"I really must go out to see his farm," said Mr. Pertell. "I believe it may be just the place for us. But I wonder what made Sandy so sad, and so much in need of money? Perhaps I can help him."

There came the incident of Pepper Sneed falling down with the lifeboat.

"Look! Look!" cried the grouchy actor. "I don't like that! It makes me ridiculous. I demand that it be taken out, Mr. Pertell!"

"Can't do it! That's the best part of the play!" laughed the manager.

"And as for me - I positively refuse to act again, if I am to be shown as a sailor, in those ridiculous white trousers!" cried Wellington Bunn.

"Very well, then, I suppose you don't care to go on the rural circuit with us," said Mr. Pertell.

"Oh - er - ah! Um! Well, you may with-hold my resignation for a time," said the Shakespearean actor, stiffly. "But it is against my principles."

"Then we are going on the rural circuit?" asked Alice, eagerly.

"Yes," the manager assured her. "This play is going to be a big success, I'm sure. I want to try a new kind now - outdoor scenes."

And that the play was a success was soon evidenced by the receipts which poured into the treasury of the Comet Film Company.

"Oh, what do you imagine it will be like - in the country?" asked Ruth of Alice, a little later, when it was definitely decided that they were to go.

"I don't know," answered Alice. "It depends on what happens."

And what did happen may be learned by reading the next volume of this series, to be called: "The Moving Picture Girls at Oak Farm; Or, Queer Happenings While Taking Rural Plays."

"Well, I'll be glad of a little rest," said Alice, one day, when they were coming from the studio, after having posed in some scenes for a little parlor drama.

"So will I," agreed Ruth. "We have been very busy these last two weeks."

"Especially since we helped Russ to get back his patent," added her sister. "And now for Oak Farm!"

"Oh, then it's been definitely decided that we are to go there?"

"Yes, Mr. Pertell said he went out there, met Sandy Apgar and arranged to use the place. We're to board there, too. I guess it will be a help to the Apgars. Mr. Pertell said they needed money. And, Ruth, he said there was some sort of a mystery out there, too."

"A mystery? What sort?"

"I don't know. We'll have to wait until we get there. Come on, let's hurry home and tell daddy."

And now, for a time, we will take leave of the Moving Picture Girls.

George Eliot
George Gissing
George MacDonald
George Meredith
George Orwell
George Sylvester Viereck
George Tucker
George W. Cable
George Wharton James
Gertrude Atherton
Gordon Casserly
Grace E. King
Grace Gallatin
Grace Greenwood
Grant Allen
Guillermo A. Sherwell
Gulielma Zollinger
Gustav Flaubert
H. A. Cody
H. B. Irving
H.C. Bailey
H. G. Wells
H. H. Munro
H. Irving Hancock
H. Rider Haggard
H. W. C. Davis
Haldeman Julius
Hall Caine
Hamilton Wright Mabie
Hans Christian Andersen
Harold Avery
Harold McGrath
Harriet Beecher Stowe
Harry Castlemon
Harry Coghill
Harry Houidini
Hayden Carruth
Helent Hunt Jackson
Helen Nicolay
Hendrik Conscience
Hendy David Thoreau
Henri Barbusse
Henrik Ibsen
Henry Adams
Henry Ford
Henry Frost
Henry James
Henry Jones Ford
Henry Seton Merriman
Henry W Longfellow
Herbert A. Giles
Herbert Carter
Herbert N. Casson
Herman Hesse
Hildegard G. Frey
Homer
Honore De Balzac
Horace B. Day
Horace Walpole
Horatio Alger Jr.
Howard Pyle
Howard R. Garis
Hugh Lofting
Hugh Walpole
Humphry Ward
Ian Maclaren
Inez Haynes Gillmore
Irving Bacheller
Isabel Hornibrook
Israel Abrahams
Ivan Turgenev
J.G.Austin
J. Henri Fabre
J. M. Barrie
J. Macdonald Oxley
J. S. Fletcher
J. S. Knowles
J. Storer Clouston
Jack London
Jacob Abbott
James Allen
James Andrews
James Baldwin
James Branch Cabell
James DeMille
James Joyce
James Lane Allen
James Lane Allen
James Oliver Curwood
James Oppenheim
James Otis
James R. Driscoll
Jane Austen
Jane L. Stewart
Janet Aldridge
Jens Peter Jacobsen
Jerome K. Jerome
John Burroughs
John Cournos
John F. Kennedy
John Gay
John Glasworthy
John Habberton
John Joy Bell
John Kendrick Bangs
John Milton
John Philip Sousa
Jonas Lauritz Idemil Lie
Jonathan Swift
Joseph A. Altsheler
Joseph Carey
Joseph Conrad
Joseph E. Badger Jr
Joseph Hergesheimer
Joseph Jacobs
Jules Vernes
Julian Hawthrone
Julie A Lippmann
Justin Huntly McCarthy
Kakuzo Okakura
Kenneth Grahame
Kenneth McGaffey
Kate Langley Bosher
Kate Langley Bosher
Katherine Cecil Thurston
Katherine Stokes
L. A. Abbot
L. T. Meade
L. Frank Baum
Latta Griswold
Laura Dent Crane
Laura Lee Hope
Laurence Housman
Lawrence Beasley
Leo Tolstoy
Leonid Andreyev
Lewis Carroll
Lewis Sperry Chafer
Lilian Bell
Lloyd Osbourne
Louis Hughes
Louis Tracy
Louisa May Alcott
Lucy Fitch Perkins
Lucy Maud Montgomery
Luther Benson
Lydia Miller Middleton
Lyndon Orr
M. Corvus
M. H. Adams
Margaret E. Sangster
Margret Howth
Margaret Vandercook

Margret Penrose
Maria Edgeworth
Maria Thompson Daviess
Mariano Azuela
Marion Polk Angellotti
Mark Overton
Mark Twain
Mary Austin
Mary Catherine Crowley
Mary Cole
Mary Hastings Bradley
Mary Roberts Rinehart
Mary Rowlandson
M. Wollstonecraft Shelley
Maud Lindsay
Max Beerbohm
Myra Kelly
Nathaniel Hawthrone
Nicolo Machiavelli
O. F. Walton
Oscar Wilde
Owen Johnson
P.G. Wodehouse
Paul and Mabel Thorne
Paul G. Tomlinson
Paul Severing
Percy Brebner
Peter B. Kyne
Plato
R. Derby Holmes
R. L. Stevenson
R. S. Ball
Rabindranath Tagore
Rahul Alvares
Ralph Bonehill
Ralph Henry Barbour
Ralph Victor
Ralph Waldo Emmerson
Rene Descartes
Rex Beach
Rex E. Beach
Richard Harding Davis
Richard Jefferies
Richard Le Gallienne
Robert Barr
Robert Frost
Robert Gordon Anderson
Robert L. Drake
Robert Lansing
Robert Lynd
Robert Michael Ballantyne
Robert W. Chambers
Rosa Nouchette Carey
Rudyard Kipling
Samuel B. Allison
Samuel Hopkins Adams
Sarah Bernhardt
Sarah C. Hallowell
Selma Lagerlof
Sherwood Anderson
Sigmund Freud
Standish O'Grady
Stanley Weyman
Stella Benson
Stella M. Francis
Stephen Crane
Stewart Edward White
Stijn Streuvels
Swami Abhedananda
Swami Parmananda
T. S. Ackland
T. S. Arthur
The Princess Der Ling
Thomas A. Janvier
Thomas A Kempis
Thomas Anderton
Thomas Bailey Aldrich
Thomas Bulfinch
Thomas De Quincey
Thomas Dixon
Thomas H. Huxley
Thomas Hardy
Thomas More
Thornton W. Burgess
U. S. Grant
Valentine Williams
Various Authors
Vaughan Kester
Victor Appleton
Victoria Cross
Virginia Woolf
Wadsworth Camp
Walter Camp
Walter Scott
Washington Irving
Wilbur Lawton
Wilkie Collins
Willa Cather
Willard F. Baker
William Dean Howells
William le Queux
W. Makepeace Thackeray
William W. Walter
William Shakespeare
Winston Churchill
Yei Theodora Ozaki
Yogi Ramacharaka
Young E. Allison
Zane Grey

www.ingramcontent.com/pod-product-compliance
Lightning Source LLC
LaVergne TN
LVHW090607110826
845146LV00001B/295

* 9 7 8 1 4 2 1 8 2 4 9 6 3 *